HARRY STYLES

THE STORIES BEHIND THE SONGS

HARRY STYLES

THE STORIES BEHIND THE SONGS

CAROLINE SULLIVAN

WELBECK

ONE DIRECTION ·

PART 1

HARRY STYLES.

PART 2

INTRODUCTION

It's possible to count on the fingers of two hands the boy-band stars who survive and thrive once the screaming stops. And only one hand is needed to tick off those who not only maintain their superstar status but also successfully take the reins of their own artistry.

In other words, those who transition into adept and confident songwriters, learn their way around the recording studio and see music not as a route to fame but as a serious vocation. There's Michael Jackson – obviously – George Michael, Justin Timberlake, Ricky Martin and ... let's add Harry Styles to the list.

While Harry's not absolutely there yet in terms of calling all the shots himself – he's still humble enough to take advice and let older heads guide when necessary – he's getting there, and it only takes a glance at his discography to appreciate how far he's come since the One Direction days. (Not that he was a slouch then – he co-wrote several tracks on each of 1D's five albums.) His name appears in the writing credits of every song on all of his solo albums – and he's been writing for other artists, too. They include Jack Antonoff's Bleachers ("Alfie's Song (Not So Typical Love Song)"), country star Cam ("Changes"), Ariana Grande ("Just a Little Bit of Your Heart") and *The X Factor USA* winners Alex & Sierra ("I Love You").

The writing credit on that last track is "Johan Carlsson/Mick Greenberg", but Greenberg has been identified by many outlets as a pen name, and the song provides clues that have led fans to believe it is indeed Harry Styles. It's been said that the subject is his brief 2012–2013 relationship with Taylor Swift, and to support that theory, both fandoms – "Harries" and "Swifties" – have pointed out that it contains a reference to romantically tracing a name on a lover's back – a detail also mentioned several years later in Taylor's 2020 song "August".

Unlike many former boy-band stars, Harry talks about One Direction, who've been on "permanent hiatus" since January 2016, in highly positive terms. He sees the UK's biggest pop group of the 21st century as a great place to have trained for the position he occupies now. "When you leave a boy band, you feel like you have to go the complete other direction and say, 'Don't worry, everyone, I hated it, it wasn't me'," he said in the 2017 documentary *Harry Styles: Behind the Album*. "[But] I loved it. I wouldn't be here if it wasn't for that band, and I don't feel like I have to apologize for that."

And what is the position he occupies now? Put it this way, he's so wildly famous that in January 2026 *The Guardian* ran a longish piece about the grammatical correctness of the title *Kiss All the Time. Disco, Occasionally.* The article reported that the comma had caused a minor social-media furore, quoting the X user Small Destructible Genius: "The comma turns the second sentence from a parallel imperative sentence to a fragment that vaguely gestures toward the occasional presence of disco."

This is the first book to focus on Harry Styles' music, from One Direction through to *Kiss All the Time.* Working through 14 years of his journey to stardom, you'll find analysis of the songs, insights from Harry and others – from fans to fellow musicians – and essays on other parts of his career, including tours and cover versions. With a focus on key 1D tracks and a deep dive into every single solo Harry Styles song, this book aims to capture the essence of the artist through his music. His progress has been remarkable, and an object lesson in never underestimating a musician. Now in his thirties – he's an Aquarian, born February 1, 1994 – he's come a very long way, but he is only just starting to show what he can do.

Opposite: Sparkling at his first Coachella headline show on April 15, 2022.

PART 1

ONE DIRECTION

65998

UP ALL NIGHT

After coming third on the seventh series of *The X Factor* (behind winner Matt Cardle and runner-up Rebecca Ferguson) on December 12, 2010, One Direction almost immediately began work on their first album. Time was of the absolute essence. If they were to stick in the minds of the public, they had to be seen and heard, but their debut also had to be a quality product. Working with the era's biggest songwriting names, from Steve Mac to Kelly Clarkson – herself a talent show winner – the band strived to make *Up All Night* the best it could be.

The boys' career arc was just beginning; released on November 18, 2011, *Up All Night* was a massive, platinum-selling hit in multiple countries. In the UK it sold 1.1 million copies, in the US 2.095 million.

It topped the charts in America – the first debut LP by a Brit band ever to hit No. 1 on *Billboard's* Top 200 chart – and in 15 other countries, too. Surprisingly, Britain wasn't one of them; Rihanna's *Talk That Talk* proved impossible to dislodge from the No. 1 spot.

Still, by the end of 2012, 1D could laugh off the failure to hit No. 1 at home – *Up All Night* had sold 4.5 million copies worldwide, making it the third-biggest-selling album of that year. The icing on the cake: in America they finished 2012 with two of the year's five best-selling albums: *Up All Night* and their second release, *Take Me Home.*

You could argue that all those sales were attributable to 1D having appeared on *The X Factor* for 12 weeks in a row, and then on the *X Factor Live* tour, followed by their own 54-date *Up All Night* tour. In other words, constant visibility had a lot to do with the album's success.

You *could* have made that argument, and some areas of the media did. In a January 11, 2012, review of the band's show at London's Hammersmith Apollo, for instance, *The Guardian*'s critic acerbically suggested that fans admired them mainly for their looks. The review began: "'Screw Bieber fever,' tweeted a fan on the afternoon of this boy band's first London headline gig, 'I've got a One Direction infection.' It sounds unappetizing, but given the lifespan of most boy bands, it probably won't last long." That critic was wrong. The "infection" lasted through the entire four years of the band's career.

In January 2011, One Direction went to Los Angeles to start making their first LP, and that's where the actual hard work began. They collaborated with super-producer/songwriter RedOne – then fresh off co-producing Lady Gaga's *Born This Way* – but after a month the boys had to leave for two months to appear on the *X Factor Tour.* While they were gone, Sonny Takhar of 1D's label, Syco Music, was scouting material for their return: "We started finding and sourcing songs and creating situations where songs were written for the boys," he told *Music Week* on August 19, 2011.

Sessions in Sweden, the US and the UK followed, with a dozen of the era's biggest pop and dance names lending their writing and production expertise, among them Savan (Ariana Grande) Kotecha and Biff (Spice Girls) Stannard. The band themselves wrote three tracks – "Taken", "Everything About You" and "Same Mistakes" – in collaboration with more-experienced names, giving them their first taste of creating songs as professionals. The sound they crafted was old-school pop – "roustabout rhythms rather than breakbeats", said *The Observer* on April 7, 2013 – and its themes were also traditional: girls, having fun, empowerment. For *Up All Night* they were rewarded with near-uniform warm reviews.

Opposite above: Promoting the *X Factor* final with Simon Cowell at a photocall/press conference. The Connaught Hotel, London, December 9, 2010.

Opposite below: Being made up for a November 13, 2010, appearance on The *X Factor*.

WHAT MAKES YOU BEAUTIFUL

SINGLE

RELEASED: SEPTEMBER 11, 2011 (SINGLE) / NOVEMBER 18, 2011 (ALBUM)
WRITERS: SAVAN KOTECHA, RAMI YACOUB, CARL FALK
PRODUCERS: RAMI YACOUB AND CARL FALK
ALTERNATE VERSIONS: *ITUNES FESTIVAL: LONDON 2012* EP, LIVE FROM SAN SIRO, *LIVE* EP

For those who hadn't been following 1D, this bubbly power-pop tune, released two months ahead of the album, was probably their first encounter with the group's music.

"What Makes You Beautiful" was not only their first single, it became a signature song for them – the one that even non-fans recognized. It sold a whopping 4.8 million and 2.4 million copies in the US and UK respectively – and because streaming didn't yet count towards sales (that started in 2014), all of those millions were "pure sales". And it's now had over 1 billion *YouTube* views.

BBC Radio 1 premiered the song on August 10, 2011, a month before release, and the band were there in the BBC studio for the occasion. The next day, Liam Payne wrote on his "Radio 1 blog": "It was the most surreal experience of my life so a BIG thankyou Radio 1, Scott and the team." The R1 play hyped up demand and, sure enough, four weeks later "What Makes You Beautiful" entered the UK chart at No. 1. In America, it reached a not-bad-at-all No. 4. (Note: in the US, release was delayed until February 2012 so it could be deployed as part of the promotional arsenal for *Up All Night*, released on March 23.)

Co-writer Savan Kotecha, who had worked on *The X Factor* as a vocal coach (though he preferred the term "vocal producer"), originally wrote the song for his wife, Anna Gustavsson, to remind her that even on days when she felt unattractive, she was always gorgeous to him. Cannily, he realized that the story would make a great plot for a song. (It's also the lyric he's proudest of having written, he told *The Hollywood Reporter* in 2013.) Once 1D recorded the track, in several sessions in Sweden and Los Angeles spread out over almost a year, the entire band knew it was a strong contender to be their first single. It was madly catchy, and in terms of sweetness and wholesomeness – qualities that the band exuded, and which made them popular both with the fandom and the fandom's parents – it could hardly be bettered. "What teenage girl does not want to hear that message [that she's beautiful even if she doesn't know it]?" asked the *New York Times* in a March 2012 story.

The single was supported by a fizzy video showing the band frolicking on a Malibu beach with three girls. Though some observers raised an eyebrow at the lyric – American talk-show host Stephen Colbert was especially scathing, saying, "Remember, girls, low self-esteem – very attractive to men" – the track was so popular with everyone else that it won the 2012 Brit Award for British Single of the Year.

hmv

GOTTA BE YOU

SINGLE

RELEASED: NOVEMBER 11, 2011 (SINGLE) / NOVEMBER 18, 2011 (ALBUM)
WRITERS: AUGUST RIGO AND STEVE MAC
PRODUCER: STEVE MAC
ALTERNATE VERSIONS: *LIVE* EP, STEVE SMART AND WESTFUNK REMIX, MOJAM REMIX

***Up All Night*'s second single was this dramatic (violins! Orchestral flourishes!) piece, which opened with Liam's lead vocal on the first verse, followed by Harry's soaring tenor on the pre-chorus, bringing us to the big, airborne chorus, on which everyone joins in.**

"It's a bit more emotive than the last one," Zayn Malik told *Digital Spy*, which was something of an understatement; where "What Makes You Beautiful" was frothy summer-pop, "Gotta Be You" felt autumnal and passionate. "I think it's going to pull a few heartstrings," Zayn added.

The emotional momentum is kept up throughout the track's 4.01 minutes, and an entire nation was able to hear it when 1D sang it on Series 8 of *The X Factor*. That performance, on November 13, 2011, is well worth seeking out because of the circularity it represents. A scant 11 months earlier, the boys had stood on the same stage, wondering what the future held. Watched by 17 million people across the UK, they'd been knocked into third place in the *X Factor* final, and mentor Simon Cowell had announced that he was "absolutely gutted" for them. But, he added presciently, "This is just the beginning for these boys."

Less than a year later, here they were – the biggest boy band in Britain *and* the States. It must have been sweet vindication for all. Cowell told ITV's *Good Morning Britain* on July 12, 2024 that he regretted not owning the One Direction name; if he did, he'd stage a digital-avatar show along the lines of Abba's hugely popular *Abba Voyage*, "and I wouldn't have to ask anyone". The band name belongs to the band themselves, meaning that no third party can put together a group including just one or two original members and send them on tour as "One Direction". Suffice to say that if the original band ever decides to reform, albeit in reduced form after the tragic death of Liam Payne in 2024, fans would go wild.

There are strong harmonies afoot on the single, and the entire thing is a swooning testament to love lost but hopefully regained. Reviewers were impressed; according to *Cosmopolitan*'s Sarah Kwong, "I have to admit it; this is brooding pop at its best." The accompanying video was likewise remarkable: 1D were dressed as preppy college boys – pullovers, chinos and all – as they wandered along the shore of Lake Placid, New York.

According to fans, Louis found the song difficult to record. It was said that he'd been told he could perform the song's second solo, but at the last minute the part was given to Harry instead. Nevertheless, he uncomplainingly did his bit on the harmonies, contributing to an excellent track that reached No. 3 in the UK chart.

Opposite: All the feels at an *X Factor Live* show, October 9, 2012.

SINGLE

ONE THING

RELEASED: JANUARY 6, 2012 (SINGLE) / NOVEMBER 18, 2011 (ALBUM)
WRITERS: SAVAN KOTECHA, RAMI YACOUB, CARL FALK
PRODUCERS: RAMI YACOUB AND CARL FALK
ALTERNATE VERSIONS: *ITUNES FESTIVAL: LONDON 2012* EP, ACOUSTIC

Videos, it needs noting, are a 1D strong point. The clip for the third single, "One Thing", is a particularly strong effort; it brings together – as their best videos do – a director with a good idea and a band willing to bring it to life.

Here, the director was Declan Whitebloom – also known for his single-take shoot of Taylor Swift's "We Are Never Ever Getting Back Together" – and the idea was to film the band having a mad day out in London, rushing from landmark to landmark as one boisterous mob. Whitebloom described it as "It's Five Go Mad in London", and so it was.

We see them quickstepping down a hill in Battersea Park, South London; singing from the top deck of a vintage Routemaster bus; bouncing around Trafalgar Square in front of a crowd of Directioners.

The band are in the highest spirits, but you have to feel sorry for them – they were dressed in lightweight jumpers (Harry and Niall) or button-down shirts, but the video was filmed on November 28, 2011, and everyone around them is wearing coats and scarves. They must have been freezing. Talk about suffering for their art. And they did: the additional video *One Thing (Behind the Scenes)* features a scene filmed at night after a full day of working, in which they collapse into each other, rub their arms and sing, "I'm really, really cold, yeah!" In the early hours of that day, Niall had faced the camera and predicted, "This is our third music video, we're here at Battersea Park – it's going to be a long day." It was.

Anyone who's seen The Beatles' film *A Hard Day's Night* or watched the old Monkees TV series will recognize the vibe Whitebloom went for: a chirpy, cheeky gang mentality in which five young men, bonded by a year of constant companionship, have the most fun possible.

The song itself had much the same hands-in-the-air feel: 3.17 minutes of shoutalong pop, bubbling five-part harmonies and an earworm of a chorus. The storyline finds them trying to win over a girl who's failed to notice them, but it honestly could have been about anything; what counts is the catchiness, which took it to No. 9 in the UK.

That chorus, by the way, had a hard-to-miss resemblance to the Backstreet Boys' 1999 smash "I Want it That Way". One Direction knew that, and they acknowledged it during at least one show. It was in Stockholm on May 8, 2013, during the *Take Me Home Tour*, and a fan had sent a Twitter request: "Can you sing Backstreet Boys' 'I Want it That Way'? Love!" What could they do but perform an impromptu version, right there onstage?

Opposite above: Harry hearts Louis while promoting the book *One Direction: Forever Young: Our Official X Factor Story*, HMV Manchester, March 7, 2011.

Opposite below: 1D plus tiny chaise longue at the BBC Teen Awards, Wembley Arena, London, on October 9, 2011.

HARRY
LOUIS.

ALBUM TRACK

TAKEN

RELEASED: NOVEMBER 18, 2011 (ALBUM)
WRITERS: TOBY GAD, LINDY ROBBINS, HARRY STYLES, LIAM PAYNE, LOUIS TOMLINSON, NIALL HORAN, ZAYN MALIK
PRODUCER: TOBY GAD

"Taken" is the first of the band's three co-writes to appear on the album, eight songs into the tracklist. They collaborated with Toby Gad and Lindy Robbins, hugely savvy old hands who between them have written for Beyoncé, Fergie from the Black Eyed Peas, David Guetta and many more.

It's essentially a Harry/Liam vocal extravaganza, with backup on the bridge from Zayn. Louis and Niall are there, too, on backing vocals – on the early songs, the pair were often assigned the backup role, much to fans' frustration. (One suggested in a *YouTube* comment, "This should be [credited to] Harry, Liam, Zayn ft. Niall and Louis".)

Producers tended to favour Harry, Liam and Zayn for the leads, judging their voices to be the strongest. Ironically, Niall later went on to coach aspiring singers on the American edition of talent show *The Voice* (he appeared in seasons 23 and 24 in 2023 and season 28 in 2025). He was more than qualified: he'd been there. And that empathy played a part in Team Niall winning all three of his coaching series – the first time any judge had won their first three.

The pace and tone of "Taken" are balladic and reflective (some critics reckoned the melody was similar to Tom Petty's "Free Fallin"), but also riven with a vein of malicious satisfaction. The narrator addresses a girl who spurned him when he declared his love, but now that he's found someone else, she realizes her mistake. It's a story as old as time, but freshened up by the evident sincerity of Harry, Liam and Zayn's vocals. One of the many reasons 1D were so deeply loved by young women was that the band were the same age as most of the fandom – when they recorded this track Harry was 17, Zayn 18, Louis 19 and both Liam and Niall either 17 or 18; their birthdays fell midway through the album recording sessions. They were going through the same learning experiences as the Directioners, so when they sang about the pain of rejection, followed by the mixed emotions roused when the song's subject begs for another chance, it was all new to both band and fans.

The narrator throws in some zingers, telling the girl that he had been so smitten by her he'd camped out in front of her house, but he now sees her for the nasty character that she is. No, he tells her, he's not dating his new girlfriend to rouse jealousy in the first girl – he's found happiness and simply isn't interested anymore.

Because the track is tucked away in the *Up All Night* tracklist, which is front-loaded with all four of its singles, "Taken" can be overlooked. Yet it emphatically deserves its place on the album.

Opposite above: Dressed to the nines at the Brit Awards. O2 Arena, London, February 21, 2012.

Opposite below: Dressed down for a show at the Brisbane Convention and Exhibition Centre. Brisbane, Australia, April 18, 2012.

MORE THAN THIS

SINGLE

RELEASED: NOVEMBER 18, 2011 (ALBUM)
WRITER: JAMIE SCOTT
PRODUCERS: BRIAN RAWLING AND PAUL MEEHAN
ALTERNATE VERSIONS: *ITUNES FESTIVAL: LONDON 2012* EP, *LIVE* EP

Every pop album needs a good weepie. "More Than This" does that job expertly on *Up All Night*. Lyrically an agonized love song addressed to a girl who had moved on to another guy, it was a complete bells-and-whistles ballad production.

There's an understated, acoustic-guitar intro that swells into a full-blown orchestral chorus, over which each band member sings increasingly emotional solo lines. All five come together on the big choruses, harmonizing strongly, and it's necessary to listen until the last few seconds, because this is when Liam lets loose with free-soaring "Yeahs" – possibly the most impressive part of the song. Each of the boys is fully on board, which isn't always the case on some of the other singles, where Louis and Niall aren't employed to their full potential and mainly sing backup.

Written by industry veteran Jamie Scott, "More Than This" was the fourth and final single from *Up All Night*, released on May 25, 2012. Unfortunately, it met the fate that befalls many singles released at the end of an album cycle: it charted at No. 86 in the UK, 49 in Australia and 39 in Ireland. (Despite the underwhelming British performance, it was eventually certified silver, signifying 200,000 units sold. That figure was a combination of streams and paid downloads.)

Reviews ranged from positive to *really* positive: *Digital Spy*'s Robert Copsey was in the former camp, noting on November 22 that the "earworm chorus" puts the song among "the best slowies to come out of boy-band land in recent years", while Movfad of *Musicboard* said, in a retrospective May 30, 2025 review, "'More Than This' hits different when you're in your feels. The vocals? Smooth. The lyrics? Emotional. The whole vibe? Peak boy band ballad energy. It's one of those underrated 1D tracks that quietly wrecks you." Not everyone loved it – American critic Zachary Houle of *PopMatters* contended on March 15, 2012, that the track "doesn't move the band much far beyond their '90s ancestors". (He had the Backstreet Boys in mind; some listeners noted a similarity to their 1998 hit "All I Have to Give".) But those who didn't love it often had good things to say about the band generally; Houle found *Up All Night* "quite appealing and surprisingly muscular" in its entirety.

Nevertheless, "More Than This" suffered from end-of-the-era promotional malaise. It was released in the same month that the band began work on the second album, and all their energies were directed towards that. They did release a 30-second clip of themselves singing the song, which aired on *Entertainment Tonight*, but it was aimed at promoting the concert DVD *Up All Night: The Live Tour*, released on May 28, three days after "More Than This".

Opposite: Harry at the Brisbane Convention and Exhibition Centre. Brisbane, Australia, April 18, 2012.

Overleaf: At the closing ceremony of the 2012 Olympic Games. Olympic Stadium, London, August 12, 2012.

TAKE ME HOME

"It's not often you encounter a new album that you can genuinely describe as phenomenal, but the adjective fits One Direction's *Take Me Home,*" wrote *Guardian* music critic Alexis Petridis the day before the record appeared in stores and online. Much depended on their second album – any pop phenomenon could land a chart-topping debut, but the sophomore LP, released November 9, 2012, was the real test: were 1D a passing fancy, or built for the long haul? The statistics speak for themselves: No. 1 in 35 countries, four million sales. Long haul, then.

One of many interesting things about *Take Me Home* is, well, its sound. On both *Up All Night* and *Take Me Home*, One Direction had exhibited a style that was highly unusual for its time.

Rather than going in the R&B/EDM direction that was all over the charts at the time, the boys had looked much further back for inspiration, which they found in the poppy new wave of the early 1980s, and which then became associated with them.

In 2012 the sound was out of place, just as the band's clothes – jumpers, plaid shirts, chinos – were, too. 1D were throwbacks, and there was no other boy band like them in the early 2010s. The group seen as their nearest rivals, The Wanted, certainly didn't look or sound like them – *their* biggest hit, the brilliant "Glad You Came", was a danceable banger. It had 2012 stamped all over it, while 1D were more a 1981 sort of phenomenon. Carl Falk, a Swede who co-wrote many *Up All Night* songs and made a substantial contribution to *Take Me Home*, summed it up to *The Independent* on April 10, 2012: "Melody is back, pop is back."

Notably, unlike almost every other pop group of the era, the 1D boys didn't dance onstage. What? No choreo?! But this approach also emphasized their pop-star-next-door ordinariness. They were, as they said themselves, "normal lads". They were good-looking but not impossibly so, talented but not intimidatingly so. You could imagine being their friend.

This was what the 1D team of producers and writers, plus the band themselves, were working with as they began to assemble *Take Me Home*. Its cover art, revealed two months before the album's release, stays with the theme of cheeky scamps. The fivesome are clustered in and around an old-style red phone box (technically it's a K6, introduced in 1935, and considered a British design icon; *Billboard* explained it to US readers as "a bright red telephone booth"); they're clambering up the side, perching on the roof and, in Niall's case, standing inside, clutching the phone receiver. Zayn is wearing a bowler hat, Harry has a black bowtie, Liam a waistcoat. The mischief and joy bring to mind the '60s Anglo-American boy band The Monkees. The box/booth itself is now on display at London's Hard Rock Café.

The stakes were incredibly high – if all went well, *Take Me Home* could establish 1D as the biggest group in the world. Simon Cowell invited top songwriters, including Savan Kotecha, Shellback and Wayne Hector to submit "potential No. 1s only", as *The Independent* reported on April 10, 2012. More than two dozen, working in teams of three or four, made the cut. Recording sessions were squeezed into three intensive months, from May to August 2012. Everyone sweated. The result: straight in at No. 1 in both the US and the UK, and three Top 10 hits, including the British chart-topper "Little Things". By the end of this album era, there was general agreement: this gang of normal lads was the biggest band in the world.

Above: Doing their thing at the 2012 MTV Video Music Awards. Staples Center, Los Angeles, September 6, 2012.

Opposite: Every inch the pop star: arriving at the 2012 MTV Music Video Awards.

LIVE WHILE WE'RE YOUNG

SINGLE

RELEASED: SEPTEMBER 28, 2012 (SINGLE) / NOVEMBER 9, 2012 (ALBUM)
WRITERS: SAVAN KOTECHA, RAMI YACOUB, CARL FALK
PRODUCERS: RAMI YACOUB AND CARL FALK
ALTERNATE VERSIONS: DAVE AUDE REMIX, THE JUMP SMOKERS REMIX

Released as the album's lead single, on September 28, 2012, "Live While We're Young" is a breezy, pop-rocky reintroduction to 1D, not that they'd really been away.

It has the joie de vivre of "What Makes You Beautiful", which isn't surprising, as both songs were written by the team of Kotecha, Falk and Yacoub. And it has a plectrum-plucked opening guitar riff that sounds quite a bit like the riff at the start of the 1982 Clash single "Should I Stay or Should I Go?" Several advance album reviews mentioned it, and the band accordingly addressed the subject in a brief video aired by BBC *Newsbeat* on the day the track appeared.

"It's a bit like ['What Makes You Beautiful'], where the opening riff sounds similar to a certain film", Harry says. (He means "Summer Nights" from *Grease*, a similarity that had been pointed out a number of times.) Then Louis raises a valid point. "I'm sure it must be quite difficult to do a unique riff now because there's been so many songs. Surely there's only so many riffs you can pull out." But Harry reveals, "It's kind of on purpose, though. It's a great riff." The praise didn't placate some Clash fans, who complained on Twitter about the injustice of a boy band apparently using a riff first played by the punk godheads – the *NME* printed a story about it on September 24, illustrating it with a '70s photo of the unsmiling quartet staring at the camera.

The track generated another semi-scandal 17 months later, when a couple in Chelsea, Michigan, complained about it being included in a choir performance at Chelsea High School. It was, so one couple told the *Ann Arbor News* in February 2014, suggestive because of references to sexting and hooking up. Four members of the choir, including their daughter, refused to sing it, but the school maintained that it didn't violate decency guidelines, and the performance went ahead with the song included. Then, on March 2, came a tweet from Louis Tomlinson, who had somehow got wind of the controversy: "I'm deeply saddened by your complaint to Chelsea High School regarding our lyrics..." It scored 96,000 likes. A second tweet, two minutes later, got 116,000 likes. A typical response tweet simply said, "SLAY, LOUIS."

With its not-entirely-subtle allusions to risqué photos and booty calls, "Live While We're Young" *was* a bit hormonal for the band, yet it was still, at its core, a vibrant pop song that reached No. 3 in both the US and the UK.

Opposite: Living while he's young? Seen here with Taylor Swift in New York on December 6, 2012. Styles has dated many famous women.

LITTLE THINGS

SINGLE

RELEASED: NOVEMBER 12, 2012 (SINGLE) / NOVEMBER 9, 2012 (ALBUM)
WRITERS: ED SHEERAN, FIONA BEVAN
PRODUCER: JAKE GOSLING
ALTERNATE VERSIONS: LIVE FROM SAN SIRO

A striking change of pace here. "Little Things", the second single from the *Take Me Home* album (released November 12, 2012), was an unadorned ballad written by Ed Sheeran and Fiona Bevan.

While 1D had sung ballads before, none had been accompanied by a video that captured them going about their business in a recording studio. It was probably a necessary move. As a "manufactured" band, 1D were – according to many people who didn't listen to their music – only there to look good, and were uninterested in the quality of the music they made. *The Guardian's* Alexis Petridis, who didn't share that opinion, explained their viewpoint: "If you're not an 11-year-old girl or the long-suffering parent of one, their [success] will remain a mystery." He added that "Little Things" was the album's most "sophisticated lyrically and emotionally" track.

Therefore, it seemed about time that the boys were shown actually making music. The clip, directed by Vaughan Arnell, who had also shot "Live While We're Young", was filmed at Sticky Studios in Windlesham, Surrey, which belonged to the track's producer (and Sheeran's mate), Jake Gosling. The finished video was shot entirely in black-and-white and showed the band sitting in a circle, acoustic guitars perched on several laps. (Niall seems completely at home picking out chords; Louis and Liam aren't bad.) Each member was also filmed in the recording booth, where the strength of each voice is evident. Harry, at the desk, moved a fader. Shooting in monochrome imparted "purity", said Arnell. It was the perfect clap-back to critics of the band.

In a behind-the-scenes clip made available a few days after the single appeared, Harry says, "This song is my favourite song on the album – I think it's important, this video, we have to kind of keep it stripped back." Liam thinks it's "possibly our most relaxing video shoot ever – we're all just chilling out". They might have been chilling, but Arnell wasn't: "... we were in the studio for over twelve hours," he told *MTV News* in November, "and I think just to sit there and kind of perform it over and over again because I was just trying to get different shots, different angles, different qualities... It was a really tough shoot because they had to keep their energy going."

The lyrics are typically Sheeran-esque, capturing the tiny things a boy might love about a special girl – freckles, her bare back, her little habits. But it also assured her that he loved *everything*, including the things she herself didn't love, such as her figure. Some critics contended that the message was an affront to female self-esteem, but the tune's prettiness, and the strong vocal delivery got them another UK chart-topper, though it only hit No. 33 in America.

Opposite above: Schmoozing with "Little Things" co-writer Ed Sheeran at the 2013 Teen Choice Awards at Gibson Amphitheatre in Hollywood, August 11, 2013.

Opposite below: Performing at Z100's Jingle Ball 2012. Madison Square Garden, New York, December 7, 2012.

SINGLE

KISS YOU

RELEASED: JANUARY 7, 2013 (SINGLE) / NOVEMBER 9, 2012 (ALBUM)
WRITERS: RAMI YACOUB, CARL FALK, SAVAN KOTECHA, SHELLBACK, KRISTIAN LUNDIN, ALBIN NEDLER, KRISTOFFER FOGELMARK
PRODUCERS: RAMI YACOUB AND CARL FALK
ALTERNATE VERSIONS: SHAROQUE REMIX

The third and final single (the second in America) from *Take Me Home* was a full 180 from "Little Things". In fact, it would have been hard to imagine a song so completely distinct from the one before.

The tune itself, which credits seven songwriters, including old buddies Savan Kotecha and Carl Falk, and well-connected Swedes Shellback and Kristian Lundin, is vibrant and zappy.

It's been categorized as power-pop, and it's easy to imagine it in a late-'70s radio playlist, alongside The Knack's "My Sharona" and Blondie's "Heart of Glass". And, as with those classics, "Kiss You" demands that you get on the dancefloor and shout along. In a track-by-track review of *Take Me Home, Billboard* identified "Kiss You" as a future single, and two months later, on January 7, 2013, the prediction came to pass.

Seriously, though, after the subdued "Little Things" what was needed was an upbeat party number, and this was it. "Kiss You" isn't "about" anything in particular apart from the flame of attraction between a boy and girl – a flame that turns into a bonfire of lust by the end, with our narrator telling the young woman that if she'd rather skip the usual getting-to-know-you steps and head straight for the main event, he's not going to stop her. "Drool" is mentioned. You get the idea.

It sounds like it was tremendous fun to sing, which was confirmed by Liam. In November he told *MTV News*, "With the album, that's the first one that we listened to and we were like, 'Yeah, we love this song.'" He probably meant that it was the first song the band listened to from the many that had been submitted for potential inclusion on the record. For every track they record, artists hear a dozen, and of those recorded, it's common for many to end up unused. In this case, the first song Liam and the others heard also became Liam's favourite. "It holds a special place in our heart for this album, and it kind of sets the tone."

The video, again directed by Vaughan Arnell, was 3.10 minutes of madcap action – its frantic pace jibed with the rush of the music – and by the end viewers would have felt both energized and slightly breathless. Arnell had concocted an homage to past youth icons and thrown in some additional funny bits, just because. For instance: they're on surfboards, and Zayn's wearing water wings; then there's the moment when they're dressed as prisoners as they recreate the Elvis film *Jailhouse Rock*. And what about Harry giving Zayn's chest a flirtatious pinch while they're on a motorbike? Really, the video is a triumph, and the song's not bad either.

Opposite: Owning the stage at the 2013 Brit Awards. 1D won the Global Success gong. 02 Arena, London, February 20, 2013.

LAST FIRST KISS

ALBUM TRACK

RELEASED: NOVEMBER 9, 2012 (ALBUM)
WRITERS: RAMI YACOUB, CARL FALK, SAVAN KOTECHA, KRISTOFFER FOGELMARK, ALBIN NEDLER, LIAM PAYNE, LOUIS TOMLINSON, ZAYN MALIK
PRODUCERS: RAMI YACOUB, CARL FALK, KRISTOFFER FOGELMARK, ALBIN NEDLER

Niall's favourite song on the album? It's this one, co-written by Liam, Louis and Zayn, as well as Savan Kotecha, Carl Falk and several others. Niall was asked about it during a Twitter Q&A session on October 22, 2012.

Using the hashtag #asknialler, he chatted with fans, one of whom was curious about which track he liked best on the as-yet-unreleased *Take Me Home*. His instant reply: "last first kiss."

Directioners already knew about Niall's own first kiss – on February 17, 2011, he'd revealed to British teen magazine *Sugarscape* that it had been with "a foreign exchange student who came over from France. But I was, like, 11". Asked if the girl was aware that he was now in a major pop group, he replied that he didn't know.

But a first kiss is a very different thing from a last first kiss. In this song, addressed to a girl who sees the narrator as only a friend, he tells her he'd like to mean more to her. He wants to ramp up the relationship, and be her last first kiss – if she would be his, she'd never have to kiss another boy. This mid-tempo guitar/keyboard number, one of three album tracks co-written by band members, has a lulling, lilting quality, especially when the five harmonize on the choruses. Harry, meanwhile, does an outstanding job with his solo lines on the pre-chorus; his vocal is such a striking blend of purity and strength that it raises the question of why he didn't make it through the *X Factor* auditions as a solo singer. ("My mum's always told me that I'm a good singer," he told Simon Cowell during the July 2010 judges' audition; the typically-Cowell reply was "Mums don't always know." In this case, Mum did know; in fact, she'd been so confident that she'd had T-shirts made for herself and Harry's sister, Gemma, and his stepdad to wear that day, which said, "We think Harry has the X Factor.")

Billboard found the track a "solid curveball", albeit not in a potential-single way. "Things get a bit more serious here with a little bit of young love in the air," the magazine said, though it wasn't outstanding enough to be released in its own right. A review on the BBC Music website confined itself to noting that the song title was reminiscent of "the names of *Sweet Valley High* novels", while *The Guardian* read rather more into it, claiming that the lyric "deals with divesting a recalcitrant girl of her maidenhood...You do wonder what parents might make of it." Whatever parents made of it, it became a Directioner favourite, and one that was always received with joy when performed on the *Take Me Home* tour.

Opposite above left: At the 2013 Brit Awards. O2 Arena, London, February 20, 2013.

Opposite above right: Harry and his biggest fan, mum Anne Cox, at a Brits after-party. Arts Club, London, February 20, 2013.

Opposite below: One Direction pick up their Global Success Award at the 2013 Brits. O2 Arena, London, February 20, 2013.

BRIT AWARDS 2013

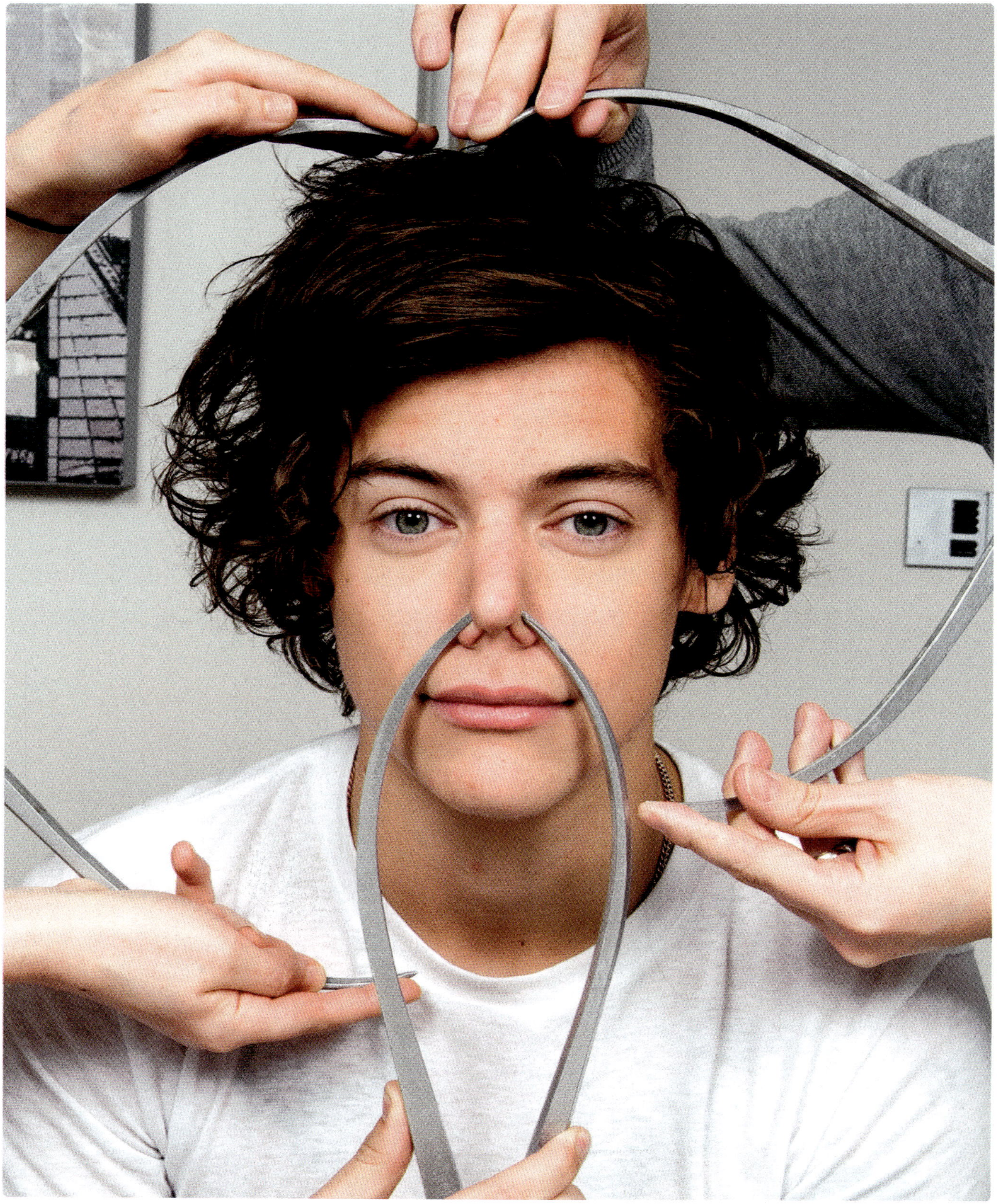

ALBUM TRACK

ROCK ME

RELEASED: NOVEMBER 9, 2012 (ALBUM)
WRITERS: SAM HOLLANDER, ALLAN GRIGG, PETER SVENSSON, HENRY WALTER, ŁUKASZ GOTTWALD
PRODUCERS: DR LUKE, KOOL KOJAK, CIRKUT, EMILY WRIGHT
ALTERNATE VERSIONS: LIVE VERSION FROM THE MOTION PICTURE "ONE DIRECTION: THIS IS US"

The four *Take Me Home* songs covered above have much to recommend them – great melodies, creamy harmonies, exceptional solo vocal performances, from Harry, Liam and Zayn especially – but what they don't have is edge. "Rock Me" is where they flipped that script.

Is it mere coincidence that the opening handclaps and percussive thuds bring to mind Queen's "We Will Rock You"? Released in 1977, the Queen classic has spent the decades since being chanted at sporting events worldwide – it hypes up crowds and has a magically inclusive effect: sing along to it and you're part of the gang.

But the introductory six seconds of "Rock Me" is as near to "We Will Rock You" as the song gets. After that, it takes another path: Harry arrives to deliver the first verse, and while the claps and beats continue, there's a different feel. This isn't a sporting anthem, it's an anthem for kicking yourself for making a big romantic mistake. But that also stirs up big, loud energy: "ROCK ME!" the song's main character begs/demands. "ROCK ME!" Drums pound, guitars blaze. When 1D played this on their *Take Me Home* and *Where We Are* tours, Liam and Niall played electric guitar, and the others hurtled around the stage, then, when it was time for Harry to sing the opening lines, he grabbed the mic stand with the imperious majesty of Freddie Mercury at Live Aid.

The storyline is that the song's main character finds himself alone after leaving a good relationship – he'd wanted to be "free", but instead he realizes he's done something stupid. Can he persuade his ex to give him another chance? He goes all-out to apologize, brooding about the good times they'd shared – he reminds her of moonlight walks on the beach and whispered endearments. He admits he was wrong to leave. He wants to do it all again. But, most of all, he wants her to rock him. So it's a heartbreak song, but it stomps. In a way, "Rock Me" was a preview of the pop-rocky sound the band would turn to on the next album, *Midnight Memories*.

Most critics were enthusiastic: *Renowned for Sound* called it "a rock-edged gem" that features "one of the tightest productions on the album", *Billboard* praised it as "a welcome deviation" from the bubblegum pop elsewhere on the record, London station Capital FM reckoned it was "one for the stadiums".

Like many good songs, it was born quickly; in this case, it took one day. Its five-strong writing team, which included Cardigans' guitarist Peter Svensson, started with the beat. American songwriter Allan Grigg "worked out a boom-boom-*wham* beat", according to *Time* magazine, while Sam Hollander came up with the title "Rock Me", after which "the melody just came".

Opposite: 1D were immortalized as waxworks in 2013 for a Madame Tussauds' travelling exhibition. Here, Harry is measured for it earlier that year.

Overleaf: Showing the Americans how it's done during a guest appearance on the *US X Factor*, December 20, 2012.

THEIR LIVES ON THE ROAD
ONE
DIRECTION
THIS IS US
PICTURE EVENT

MIDNIGHT MEMORIES

It's true that *Midnight Memories* didn't reach the top of every chart – in Italy it only managed No. 3. (The band would return to a global clean sweep of No. 1s with the next album, *Four*.) But the expression "You win some, you lose some" applies here. *Midnight Memories* may have lost Italy, but it won some of the best reviews of their career, and it took One Direction in a rocky new (sorry!) direction. And although it was released late in the year, on November 25, 2013, it became the world's highest-selling album of 2013, at 4 million sales.

While making the record, Liam was highly optimistic about the band's new rock sound – so much so that he had the first four words to the track "You & I" tattooed on his right forearm. It was inked in August 2013, and its placement on the arm, next to a feather he'd acquired four months earlier, was significant.

The feather represented his grandmother, who had died when he was young; one day soon after, he found "this huge feather", he told *GQ* in September 2019. Because he'd recently read a story about a little boy finding owl feathers around his house, he explained, "me and my mum kind of thought it was my nan". Thus, his getting the "You & I" tattoo next to it was meaningful.

Interestingly, that song was one of only three on *Midnight Memories* that the band had no part in writing. At least one member is credited on each of the other 11 tracks, so it's noteworthy that Liam chose one of the others. Moreover, his choice was a ballad – a ballad on the record that otherwise sought to break *away* from ballads and cute-guy pop.

Midnight Memories did its job, and then some – it was so successful at moving the music forward and giving more creative control to the group that even critics who'd been negative about the previous records found good things to say. "The tunes may still go a little heavy on the sugar, but it's no longer strictly gooey, syrupy teen pop," offered the *Arts Desk* on November 28. "Who would have predicted the triumphant power chords of the title track?"

Who indeed? Well, the band themselves would have. "We take our music so seriously," Louis said in a pre-release interview with ABC's *Nightline*. "And especially this [new] record… we have done a lot of writing on it. For us, the music is such an important part."

It was mainly made during late-night writing and recording sessions – hence "midnight" – and the majority of those took place during the February–November 2013 *Take Me Home* tour. Because they were on the road, writing and recording sessions took place wherever they found themselves, including tour buses and hotels. Recording studios were set up in hotel rooms. And, according to regular writer Savan Kotecha (who played a smaller part on this record), it was Louis who guided them "away from the very poppy stuff of the first two albums. He was leading the charge to make sure that they had a more mature sound," he told *Rolling Stone* in a July 2020 article titled "How One Direction Became One of the Best Rock Bands of the 21st Century".

Julian Bunetta, whose writing and production work are prominent on the album, said in the same article, "This was a make-or-break moment for them. They needed to grow up, or they were gonna go away – and they wanted to grow up." Thus, with this record, One Direction secured their future.

Above: At a photocall for the concert film *One Direction: This Is Us* at Big Sky Studios, London, August 19, 2013.

Opposite: Harry and Miley Cyrus pose backstage at the 2013 Teen Choice Awards at Gibson Amphitheatre in Hollywood, August 11, 2013.

Canon
Canon

TEENAGE
INSERT COIN
KICKS
UP TO 5 CAN PLAY

BEST SONG EVER

SINGLE

RELEASED: JULY 22, 2013 (SINGLE) / NOVEMBER 25, 2013 (ALBUM)
WRITERS: WAYNE HECTOR, JOHN RYAN, JULIAN BUNETTA, ED DREWITT
PRODUCERS: JULIAN BUNETTA, JOHN RYAN, MATT RAD
ALTERNATE VERSIONS: SMART AND WESTFUNK REMIX, KAT KRAZY REMIX

Between the end of the *Take Me Home* era and the start of the *Midnight Memories* cycle, 1D had a No. 1 UK single with an energetic medley of Blondie's "One Way or Another" and The Undertones' "Teenage Kicks".

Released on February 13, 2013, it was their contribution to the annual Red Nose Day charity fundraiser in the UK. It ended up being the 24th-biggest-selling single of 2013, and, rather surprisingly, was the only One Direction single to make it into the year's Top 40. Its video is still worth a watch, if only for the scenes featuring then-Prime Minister David Cameron.

We see him opening the door to 10 Downing Street to find out who's making all that noise on the front steps; upon seeing One Direction, he rolls his eyes with a "They don't pay me enough for this" look on his face.

The *Midnight Memories* era proper began on July 22, 2013, with the appearance of its first single, "Best Song Ever" – one of the few songs that included no writing contribution from the band. In an interview on BBC Radio 1 on July 19, Harry pronounced it "my favourite song that we've done so far... coming back with new music, this is a bit different from what we've done before. It's a bit heavier. We're not Slipknot or anything, but the drums are bigger, the guitars are bigger."

Quite so – many reviewers heard a touch of The Who's very-big-indeed 1971 classic, "Baba O'Riley", in the track's structure. An internet rumour took flight: supposedly, The Who were planning legal action over the resemblance. The Who guitarist/songwriter Pete Townshend was compelled to address furious Directioners: "I like the single. I like One Direction," he said in a statement issued in August 2013. "The chords I used and the chords they used are the same three chords we've all been using in basic pop music."

Titling the track "Best Song Ever" was a brave decision – except that the lyric made it clear that nobody was claiming *this* was the world's best song; in fact, it was about meeting a bewitching girl called Georgia Rose at a club, and spending the night dancing with her – such a heady experience that the narrator decides that whatever tune they danced to must have been the best one ever.

The song's video was an absolute must-see: it featured the band both as themselves and as heavily made-up and bewigged American record executives. Each played a hilariously stereotypical character – Zayn was "sexy assistant" Veronica, Harry the eager marketing manager Marcel, Liam the wildly flamboyant choreographer Leroy, while Louis and Niall play studio executives called Jonny and Harvey, respectively. Cool track, great video – no wonder "Best Song Ever" hit No. 2 in both the UK and US charts.

Opposite above: Playing around on NBC's *Today*. Rockefeller Plaza, New York, August 23, 2013.

Opposite below: Storming through the No. 1 single "One Way or Another (Teenage Kicks)" at the Brit Awards. 02 Arena, London, February 20, 2013.

STORY OF MY LIFE

SINGLE

RELEASED: OCTOBER 28, 2013 (SINGLE) / NOVEMBER 25, 2013 (ALBUM)
WRITERS: JAMIE SCOTT, JULIAN BUNETTA, JOHN RYAN, HARRY STYLES, LIAM PAYNE, LOUIS TOMLINSON, NIALL HORAN, ZAYN MALIK
PRODUCERS: JULIAN BUNETTA AND JOHN RYAN
ALTERNATE VERSIONS: LIVE FROM SAN SIRO, LIVE X FACTOR PERFORMANCE

If Harry's favourite *Midnight Memories* track was "Best Song Ever", this – the second single, released October 28, 2013 – was Niall's. "It's up there with the best that we've brought out, but 'Story of My Life' might just take it," he said on London's Capital FM a few days before release. "It's a very passionate song."

It *is* passionate, if passion is judged by the depth of feeling in the singers' voices. From the first verse, sung by Harry and Liam, the emotion is palpable, almost touchable; it's plain that the words mean something to them. The words themselves are not extraordinary – they tell a story encountered in other 1D songs, wherein a young man fears that his adored girlfriend no longer loves him. Again, what sells the lyric, and the song itself, is the understated ache in the voices.

"Story of My Life" dates back to March 20, 2013, when the *Take Me Home* tour touched down at Nottingham's Capital FM Arena (now the Motorpoint Arena). Their frequent writing collaborator Jamie Scott was in the city with them, and that night he wanted to play them a song he'd come up with. It was a slam dunk. "We just fell in love with it the second we heard it," Niall said. By the time it was recorded, the band had contributed to the lyric themselves, a process Scott considered vital to ensure that "they're really singing what they're singing about".

The demo Scott played for them in Nottingham had a folk ambience that was tangible in the recorded version, though Scott himself felt that, due to the effect of 1D's distinctive harmonizing voices, the track was now simply a One Direction song rather than a folk number. That failed to stop many reviewers from noting an underlying rootsiness, and several were reminded of Mumford & Sons. Whatever the song's genre, it was the first 1D single to win wide critical acclaim; some reviewers, like *Idolator*'s Sam Lansky, claimed to be surprised by "how sincerely *great*" it was. It was a "more mature midpoint" between their customary pop and balladry. "With that song, I feel like we lifted them to another level," Scott told *The Guardian* on September 23, 2016.

The video, too, was more touching than usual. The band are shown in a photo lab, developing pictures that turn out to be actual photos from their childhood. In them, each future One Directioner poses with a family member – Harry with mum Anne, Zayn with sister Waliyha, Liam with his parents and sisters, Niall with his brother and Louis with his grandparents. Each member then recreates the same pose with his family as they are today, a poignant idea that works beautifully. The song reached No. 2 in the UK, 9 in the US.

Opposite above: 1D attend the New York premiere of *One Direction: This is Us* at the Ziegfeld Theatre, August 26, 2013.

Opposite below: At the MTV Video Music Awards at the Barclays Center, Brooklyn, New York, on August 25, 2013.

SONY

MIDNIGHT MEMORIES

SINGLE

RELEASED: MARCH 9, 2014 (SINGLE) / NOVEMBER 25, 2013 (ALBUM)
WRITERS: JULIAN BUNETTA, JAMIE SCOTT, JOHN RYAN, LOUIS TOMLINSON, LIAM PAYNE
PRODUCERS: JAMIE SCOTT, JULIAN BUNETTA, JOHN RYAN

The album's title track, released on March 9, 2014, is a straightforward, no-pussyfooting story of being a touring band – a touring band who somehow show up at your house party, find it dull, then hare off to start a party of their own at the local kebab shop.

It turns into a rip-roaring good time, with dozens of people crammed into the shop, singing the chorus along with One Direction.

But wait, there's more: post-kebab, they make off with pensioners' mobility scooters, "borrow" a Thames River Police boat and finish the night precariously balanced on a narrow ledge that runs the length of London's Tower Bridge. (It goes without saying: don't try any of this at home.)

This highly watchable screen action unfolds during the video, but there's a bonus: the song rocks like nothing they'd recorded before. There were frequent comparisons in the media to Def Leppard – specifically, the veteran Brit-metal band's 1987 US No. 2 hit, "Pour Some Sugar on Me". Did that matter? Not to Def Leppard. As with Pete Townshend not caring that "Best Song Ever" might bear a glancing resemblance to The Who's "Baba O'Riley", Def Leppard guitarist Vivian Campbell weighed in to tell *Billboard* that it was "very flattering that all of a sudden these kids think it's a cool sound".

According to Liam, "Midnight Memories" was the first song written for their third album. Speaking to Ryan Seacrest on iHeart Radio on the album's release day, he revealed that once the song was finished – he wrote it with Louis, Julian Bunetta, Jamie Scott and John Ryan – "it set us on course of what writing the rest of this album was going to be". And because most of the album was created while they were touring – they even used hotel rooms as recording studios, upending mattresses against walls as soundproofing – Niall added that the process was driven by having an inflexible schedule.

In *Rolling Stone*'s July 22, 2020, piece, which appeared the day before the tenth anniversary of 1D becoming a band, Bunetta revealed that the majority of *Midnight Memories* – including the title track – came together in London in early 2013, rather than on the road, as had been generally thought. Bunetta, John Ryan, Jamie Scott, Wayne Hector and Ed Drewett spent just over a week workshopping ideas with the band in London; then, armed with the basic song structures, One Direction headed out on the *Take Me Home* tour, where they fine-tuned them.

And those on-the-road sessions gave *Midnight Memories* its name; most of it gelled between midnight and five in the morning. Curiously, given the title track's excellence, it only reached 39 in the UK, but it fared better elsewhere, hitting No. 12 in America.

Opposite: Dressed for a frigid New York day at Rumsey Playfield in Central Park. New York, November 26, 2013.

YOU & I

SINGLE

RELEASED: APRIL 18, 2014 (SINGLE) / NOVEMBER 25, 2013 (ALBUM)
WRITERS: JULIAN BUNETTA, JAMIE SCOTT, JOHN RYAN
PRODUCERS: JULIAN BUNETTA AND JOHN RYAN
ALTERNATE VERSIONS: PIANO VERSION, DUET, RADIO EDIT, BIG PAYNO REMIX

In terms of chart action, the album's fourth and final single, released April 18, 2014, suffered from the apparent public indifference that plagues any number of tracks released at the end of an album cycle.

As a point of comparison, Janet Jackson's 1986 blockbuster *Control* yielded seven singles over nearly two years, and the sixth, "The Pleasure Principle", only got as far as No. 14 in the US. The final release, "Funny How Time Flies (When You're Having Fun)", was released solely for airplay in the US – a gambit to keep an artist visible when everyone already owns their current album and there are no more viable full-release singles.

That being the case, perhaps it wasn't surprising that "You & I" just scraped into the Brit Top 20, at 19, while its American showing – 68 – would turn out to be the worst performance of a 1D single there.

The chart outcome was a little unfair, because "You & I" was what every boy-band-turned-pop-rock-outfit needs in their arsenal: a credible power ballad. It hit the same sort of emotional summits and drops as Snow Patrol's "Chasing Cars" and Coldplay's "Fix You" without sounding like them, and deserves the adjective "massive". Written by the Bunetta/Ryan/Scott team, who were behind five other tracks on *Midnight Memories*, the tune begins pensively, with subdued solos from Niall and Liam, after which Harry comes in on the chorus and the song begins to build. Its high point – literally – is Zayn's power scream at 2.58 minutes. He produces another sustained high note from 3.28 that leads into the fade. It's quite a track.

Compared to these fireworks, the lyric plays it safe: a young couple reassure each other that they'll always be together because they're different from the rest; their love makes them special. In a behind-the-scenes video filmed alongside the main video on March 24, Harry summed it up: "You're inseparable, nothing can get in the way of you and your love." It's a lovely sentiment, but power ballads need a more dramatic declaration as their central pillar. "Chasing Cars" contains a good example: it likens a couple's love to a flowering garden, and the narrator finds himself lost in his lover's beautiful eyes.

But that didn't really matter. What did was that One Direction proved they could make a power ballad – and new doors thus opened for them. A flurry of critical praise – Tim Sendra of *Allmusic* singled out the band's "sure-handed way with a big ballad" – showed that they were now accepted as musicians. And, as a bonus, on May 23 a *You & I* EP was released. There were four tracks, offering different versions of the song, including a Big Payno Remix.

Opposite: At the 2013 American Music Awards, where 1D won in two categories. Nokia Theatre, Los Angeles, November 24, 2013.

PROMOTIONAL SINGLE

DIANA

RELEASED: NOVEMBER 18, 2013 (PROMO SINGLE) / NOVEMBER 25, 2013 (ALBUM)
WRITERS: JULIAN BUNETTA, JAMIE SCOTT, JOHN RYAN, LOUIS TOMLINSON, LIAM PAYNE
PRODUCERS: JULIAN BUNETTA AND JOHN RYAN

"Diana" was a promotional single that was leaked online on September 24, 2013, and "officially" released a week before the album, on November 18. The rules around promo singles are confusing.

As releases, they primarily exist to fuel excitement for an upcoming album and generally don't receive the push that official singles do. In some cases, they're not chart-eligible.

In this case, "Diana" was gifted to people who'd pre-ordered *Midnight Memories* (as were "Story of My Life", the album's title track and "You & I"). But while it wasn't an official single, it did receive an official release – go figure that one out – and on that first day it leapt to No. 1 on iTunes charts around the world. It also made No. 58 in the UK Official Singles Chart, and 11 on the US *Billboard* Hot 100 (it dropped off both countdowns a week later).

Co-written by Louis, Liam and Bunetta/Ryan, this '80s-influenced pop-rocker was jauntily optimistic, if you didn't read the lyrics. The words made it clear that it was directed at someone – a girl called Diana – who was depressed; the singers assured her that she wasn't alone, that they would try to support her. Movingly, it went on to say that her support for them was saving *them*; that the love she lavished on One Direction helped them to cope with their own lives.

But there was more to the story. The song was about a real young woman whose name may have been Joanna. At least, according to Louis, "Joanna" was what they were working with while writing: "[But it's] actually quite close to my mum's name [Johannah], and it felt a little weird so we changed it to Diana," he told *Perez TV*. Bunetta confirmed in an MTV News interview that the subject was indeed a real person. "It's definitely about somebody. Maybe one day somebody will tell. But we can't tell."

Online talk among Directioners suggested that in a letter to Niall Horan – whom she had apparently never met – Diana had written of her deep depression, and eventually took her own life. That version seemed to be substantiated by Bunetta. "I think that the lyric probably pertains to what a lot of the fans are going through... People feel like they're alone and [their escape is] Twitter and [finding] people that also relate to them." The song was a way of letting others in the same state know they were seen and heard. "Diana," he said, was "a ...pretty accurate depiction of the loneliness someone can feel in such a huge world and someone saying 'Hey, I feel you. I know you're there. I notice you; it's OK. You're not alone.'" Whatever the real story is, it makes for a powerful addition to the band's catalogue.

Opposite: Onstage at the iHeartRadio Music Festival. MGM Grand Garden Arena, Las Vegas, September 20, 2014.

Overleaf: Feigning surprise at winning the Brits Global Success award for the second time. 02 Arena, London, February 19, 2014.

#BRITs2014
BRITs.co.uk
BRIT AWARDS 2014
with MasterCard

#BRITs2014
BRITs.co.uk
#BRITs2014
MasterCard
TONE

FOUR

Many a killjoy predicted that One Direction wouldn't last beyond their first album, yet here they were with album number four, handily titled *Four*. The name was picked not just to mark its place in their catalogue, but to celebrate four years as a band. Their 1D Media Limited company turned over £73.7 million in 2014, yet their dedication to music – not money – was growing with every release. With almost half a decade of hands-on experience, 1D were coming into their own as songwriters, and on *Four* they found their feet as assured makers of indie-pop and stadium rock.

During a #FOURHANGOUT Google livestream on November 9, 2014, host Ben Winston (director of several of their videos and the 2011 TV film, *One Direction: A Year in the Making*) asked Niall, "What's the difference between now and when it first started?" He replied, "The scale of everything is a lot bigger than it was at the start."

That word, "scale", also applied to the trajectory and shape of their music. Where the first two albums were dominated by joyous new-wave pop, and the third dipped a toe in power-chordage, now they were exploring more prominent guitar lines and propulsive AOR rock. Some reviews even noted that a few tracks were reminiscent of Bruce Springsteen. ("... an unlikely comparison," wrote the *Daily Telegraph*'s stunned reviewer on November 7.)

Another step forward was the band's actively forging their own musical identity. Louis and Liam were now an assured writing duo. While every band member racked up writing credits on *Four*, the pair were emerging as the predominant force. Their contribution to lead single "Steal My Girl", for example, resulted in an arena-rocker that was simply undeniable. Its chorus was up there, in terms of unquenchable catchiness, with arena titans like Journey and Foreigner. And the naysayers who'd slammed their early albums were now either admitting they'd been wrong, or at least no longer slamming. One Direction had weathered the critical storms, and by dint of incredibly hard work and a passion for music, they had prevailed. *Four* was proof.

Once again, a good chunk of the 12 songs on the album were recorded while on the road with the *Where We Are* tour in 2014. It was a 69-show, all-stadium trot around Europe and the Americas, running from April to October, and the schedule allowed little time off. There were windows in late July and early September, but much of the work would have to be done, again, in hotel rooms. On April 27, 2014, the day 1D's press team announced that album number four was now in the works, the band were playing the Estadio Nacional in Lima. They'd just come from Bogota, and next were Santiago, Buenos Aires, Montevideo ...

"We're doing the recording process the same as we did last year," said Niall in *One Direction: The TV Special*, aired December 23, 2014, on America's NBC network. "[Last time] we set up two mattresses against the wall, and then a microphone, a laptop, a couple of speakers and away we go." Co-producer John Ryan said, "It's better than doing it in a proper recording studio, 'cos it's more organic, every hotel room's different." Proving that very thing, there's a scene in which Harry is recording "Where Do Broken Hearts Go", composed by him, Julian Bunetta and three others. He's in a makeshift booth next to a TV, and Bunetta is sprawled on a bed, tracking the vocal on a laptop. Harry exerts himself, his voice soaring, and Bunetta smiles. "You did something so good." Result: an album that hit No. 1 around the world.

Opposite: Posing with fans at the ARIA Awards 2014 at the Star Event Centre. Sydney, Australia, November 26, 2014.

STEAL MY GIRL

SINGLE

RELEASED: SEPTEMBER 29, 2014
WRITERS: JULIAN BUNETTA, JOH
DREWITT, LOUIS TOMLINSON, LIA
PRODUCERS: JULIAN BUNETTA,
ALTERNATE VERSIONS: ACOUST
RAIDERS OF THE LOST ART REMIX

There's a science to planning the release strategy for a major record. It's known as "the plot" – "What's the plot?" a record label marketing director will ask an A&R manager, which translates as "What are the release dates, how much promo can the artist be roped into doing, can we get them onto That Cool TV Show, should we put out Track A or Track B as the lead single?"

There are many more questions along those lines, as the label liaises with band management and works out how to get the most mileage out of the upcoming record, which itself was the subject of a dozen meetings while it was being created.

Four's global release date had been decided – November 17, 2014 – and "Steal My Girl" was designated the first single. It became available everywhere on September 29 – except in Britain, where it didn't emerge until October 12. Why? That was part of the plot, too. The extra fortnight gave the band and track producers Bunetta/Ryan/Par Westerlund time to create "exclusive bonus material" in the form of a B-side. "Big Payno and AFTERHRS Pool Party Remix", as it was called – Payno was, of course, Liam, and AFTERHRS were a production duo who got involved with the track – was quite a step away from the verse/chorus/verse structure of the original "Steal My Girl". What Big Payno and AFTERHRS created was an authentic EDM club track.

The standard version of the song was anything but clubby. "Dynamic arena-pop" is the best description. Payno, Louis and five other writers, including th
Bunetta, came up with the
effective pop-rocker that
concept of it, anyway. Juli
on everybody's experience
all been in love before and
at hiding it than others, bu
girlfriends." (Presumably,
fans would relate, too, bec
steal 1D's fanbase]".

Despite the two-week de
in the US. (Despite not bre
song still sold 500,000 cop
by a fantastic video, this t
director, who takes the gr
The nonplussed band, star
to destroy [their] inhibitio
involved. It's magnificent.

Opposite above: The 2014 American Music Awards. Nokia Theatre, Los Angeles, November 23, 2014.

Opposite below: Every man goes through a hat phase. This was Harry's. American Music Awards, November 23, 2014.

NIGHT CHANGES

SINGLE

RELEASED: NOVEMBER 14, 2014 (SINGLE) / NOVEMBER 17, 2014 (ALBUM)
WRITERS: JULIAN BUNETTA, JOHN RYAN, JAMIE SCOTT, HARRY STYLES, LOUIS TOMLINSON, LIAM PAYNE, NIALL HORAN, ZAYN MALIK
PRODUCERS: JULIAN BUNETTA, JAMIE SCOTT, JOHN RYAN
ALTERNATE VERSIONS: LIVE ACOUSTIC SESSION, AFTERHRS REMIX

The video for "Night Changes", the slow jam released as *Four*'s second and final single on November 14, 2014, marked the end of an era for One Direction, though they didn't know it then.

It was the last band video Zayn would appear in, and the last single he sang on. By the time 1D's fifth album appeared, he had long since left the group. In his first major radio interview, in January 2016, he told Beats 1 presenter Zane Lowe, "From the first year, I never really wanted to be there in the band."

When he left, on March 25, 2015, every Directioner would have re-watched the video (which has now reached one billion views) for signs that Zayn was unhappy. Nothing was apparent; the first member to appear onscreen, singing the first three lines, Zayn did his bit professionally, playing a smitten boyfriend meeting his crush for dinner.

Directed, as usual, by Ben Winston, the clip followed band members as they took their squeezes on five very different sorts of date activities: Harry offered ice skating, Niall a cosy night at home with Monopoly, a visit to a fairground with Liam, a ride in Louis' snazzy sportscar and spaghetti in a fancy restaurant with Zayn. As this is a 1D video, comic moments were compulsory: Harry slips on the ice and breaks his arm, the fire sets Niall's shirt alight, Liam is sick after riding a waltzer, Louis is arrested for breaking the speed limit and Zayn has a plate of spaghetti dumped on his head by his date's ex-boyfriend. Each of those slapstick turnabouts is the moment the "night changes" into something other than a romantic evening.

The song it accompanies, however, is a sober meditation on the passing of time, and how quickly people grow up. The changes that happen on those date nights can be seen as a compressed version of the way the years rush past until people find themselves looking back from the vantage point of adulthood. In an October 2014 interview, Harry revealed to Radio 1 that it was his favourite song on the album.

Written by all five members and Scott/Bunetta/Ryan, "Night Changes" came by its name in an unexpected way. The song was being tinkered with at Jamie Scott's home studio, and one night he left the session early to look after his young child. While he was gone the others kept working, and when Scott returned several hours later, "three songs that I thought were sounding amazing when I left had been changed drastically through the night", including that one, he told *MTV News* on October 30. Those "night changes" gave their name to the song.

Opposite: Arriving at the NRJ Music Awards in Cannes, France, on December 13, 2014. 1D won International Group of the Year.

FIREPROOF

PROMOTIONAL SINGLE

RELEASED: SEPTEMBER 8, 2014 (PROMO SINGLE) / NOVEMBER 17, 2014 (ALBUM)
WRITERS: JULIAN BUNETTA, JAMIE SCOTT, JOHN RYAN, LOUIS TOMLINSON, LIAM PAYNE
PRODUCERS: JULIAN BUNETTA AND JOHN RYAN

"Fireproof" was offered as a free download for 24 hours on September 8, 2014 – a little aperitif intended to stoke excitement about the main course: *Four*.

The album's release date, November 17, was announced the same day. "Because you've supported us so much, we wanted to give a little something back," said Niall in the announcement video. "We're really proud of [the album], and we hope you won't mind us sharing a track with you right now, for free, on our website," Harry went on.

The fandom didn't need to be asked twice. In the short time that "Fireproof" was available, it was downloaded 1.1 million times, and Twitter reported 1.7 million tweets about it that day. Because major acts rarely offered free songs, it was difficult to compare like for like, but *Billboard* said that iTunes' Free Single of the Week – a promotional device that ran between 2004 and 2014 – was downloaded around 300,000 times each week on average.

The *Four* campaign included five more "free" downloads – "free" when the album was pre-ordered, that is. In order: "Ready to Run" (November 6), "Where Do Broken Hearts Go" (November 10), "18" (November 11), "Girl Almighty" (November 12) and "Fool's Gold" (November 13). But it was "Fireproof" that caused the most social-media commotion and chatter among Directioners.

Musically, "Fireproof" was an ambling, mid-tempo love song that was easy to like. *The Guardian*'s Michael Cragg described it on September 10 as a "lilting, MOR ballad" boosted by "some lovely harmonies [that] herald a breezy, 70s, soft rock-esque chorus", and other reviewers found it just as palatable. In a nobody-would've-predicted-it gesture, the October 14, 2025, edition of *Rolling Stone* Australia, arbiter of musical hipness, made "Fireproof" No. 126 in its list of The 250 Greatest Songs of the 21st Century So Far – one place behind Kelis' mighty "Milkshake".

Though its subject was the enduring, "fireproof" love between two people, "Fireproof" was the result of Liam surviving an actual fire in September 2013. The balcony of his 34th-floor apartment in London's Canary Wharf was badly damaged when a patio heater went up in flames. Liam tried to beat out the flames with his hands, and he and friend Andy Saunders were both burned. Andy spent a week in hospital, but Liam's own injuries were minor. He was able to meet his bandmates the next day, and, explaining how he'd come away nearly unscathed, told them he must be fireproof. That one word sparked a song.

Opposite above: Playing a sold-out Levi's Stadium, Santa Clara, California, halfway through the *On the Road Again* tour. July 11, 2015.

Opposite below: Presenting an award (to an absent Sam Smith) during the *Billboard* Music Awards in Las Vegas, May 17, 2015.

WHERE DO BROKEN HEARTS GO

PROMOTIONAL SINGLE

RELEASED: NOVEMBER 10, 2014 (PROMO SINGLE) / NOVEMBER 17, 2014 (ALBUM)
WRITERS: HARRY STYLES, JULIAN BUNETTA, ALI TAMPOSI, THEODORE GEIGER, RUTH-ANNE CUNNINGHAM
PRODUCERS: JULIAN BUNETTA, THEODORE GEIGER, PÄR WESTERLUND

The second download in the series of five given away with pre-orders of *Four*, the arena-rocking "Where Do Broken Hearts Go" was written by a team of five, of whom Harry was the only band member. Because of this, some speculated that he must have mined his own love life for subject matter.

The site *Bustle* ran an entire piece to that effect, suggesting that his November 2012–January 2013 relationship with Taylor Swift inspired this song, just as her own *1989* album was thought by some to be about Harry. (Well, it did feature a song called "Style", and another track, "Out of the Woods", mentions a snowmobile accident said to have involved the pair of them.)

The lyric doesn't reveal much, either. It addresses a former lover who, in the mind of the narrator, is obviously the one who got away. He himself ended the relationship, and now bitterly regrets doing so; in fact, it's the worst thing he's ever done, far outranking every other "crime" he's ever committed ("crime" is artistic licence, used here to emphasize his pain). He wonders if she's since found someone else, and his jealousy boils over as he asks whether – and this really is none of his business – she's in bed with another man. Will she ever come back to the one who truly loves her? Because the point of a heartbreak song like this one is that the guilty party suddenly finds clarity and realizes that he'd loved her all along.

It was hard to believe that, as some claimed, this was an answer track motivated by "Style" and "Out of the Woods" (which became *1989*'s third and sixth singles). For one thing, *1989* was released in October 2014, so Harry wouldn't have heard those songs until well after he'd written "Where Do Broken Hearts Go". During the #FOURHANGOUT livestream, he was asked about Taylor having possibly written about him. Looking uncomfortable, he said 1D themselves write about personal experiences; thus, it would be hypocritical to stop her doing the same. "*And* she's really good, so I'm lucky in that sense," he added.

For his part, Niall loved the tune, saying, "I think 'Where Do Broken Hearts Go' is perfect." Zayn concurred: "It's a song I'd be proud to hear on the radio, and [I'd] be, like, 'Yeah, that's our band'." Niall had a particular reason for considering it perfect: the *Four* sleevenotes credit him as the guitarist on the track. He had become a capable player, able to hold his own among guitarists with decades more experience – such as Rolling Stone Ronnie Wood, who played alongside Niall when 1D performed the song on *The X Factor* 2014 finale.

Opposite: Styles causes fireworks at the Allianz Stadium in Sydney, Australia, on February 7, 2015.

ILLUSION

ALBUM TRACK

RELEASED: NOVEMBER 17, 2014 (*FOUR: THE ULTIMATE EDITION*)
WRITERS: JULIAN BUNETTA, JAMIE SCOTT, JOHN RYAN, LIAM PAYNE
PRODUCERS: JULIAN BUNETTA AND JOHN RYAN

"There's a song about Sophia, and I didn't write it, which is a bit weird," Liam told Ben Winston during the Google Hangout. He was referring to "Illusion" (track 14 on the 18-track *Four – Ultimate Edition* version of the album).

Sophia Smith was Liam's girlfriend; "Illusion" was an arena-ready rocker that asked whether she believed in their love as much as he did. At the time of the November 2014 Hangout, they'd been dating for 17 months, and were so serious that they'd discussed marriage, he said in an *Attitude* cover story in October 2015.

He was on the cover solo, thanks to having won the magazine's Sexiest Man of the Year award. Liam had been nervous about doing the interview alone and admitted that he might not have agreed without Sophia's encouragement. "She helps me through things. I love her to pieces. I've fancied the pants off her since I was at school with her."

Sadly, the couple split soon after the interview appeared, apparently at his instigation – they'd spent most of 2015 apart because of One Direction's eight-month *On the Road Again* tour, and Liam felt that continuing the relationship would have been unfair to Sophia. (Within two months, he'd become romantically involved with Cheryl Cole, while Sophia would marry in 2025.)

But at the time of the Google Hangout, their feelings for each other were so strong that the song "Illusion" was born. Liam explained how it happened. He was in the studio with the rest of the group and they'd just finished the melody to this as-yet-unnamed track. Julian Bunetta was there, and asked Liam if they could have a word outside. "He was feeling a bit low about something, and I brought my situation to him about what I was saying about what happened with me [in the relationship with Sophia]." Liam went home after that, and a bit later got a call from Bunetta, who announced, "Hey, man, we wrote the whole song about you and Soph!" Liam was a bit knocked for six: "I hadn't heard it yet, so [it] was all strange." Sophia was actually with Liam when Bunetta called, and when she heard the song, she loved it, to her boyfriend's relief.

In a spirit of blokey silliness, during the Hangout, the rest of 1D claimed the lyric had been written by Niall, and the media ran with that story. Their inference was that there must be a love triangle, and that idea gained so much traction that Liam tweeted on November 11, 2014: "Just to clear things up niall didn't write illusion that was a quick joke as that would b very strange [it] was Julian 'Jesus' Bunetta."

Opposite: Lost in music. Levi's Stadium, Santa Clara, California, on July 11, 2015.

Overleaf: Harry sings "Where Do Broken Hearts Go" at the Allianz Stadium in Sydney, Australia, February 7, 2015.

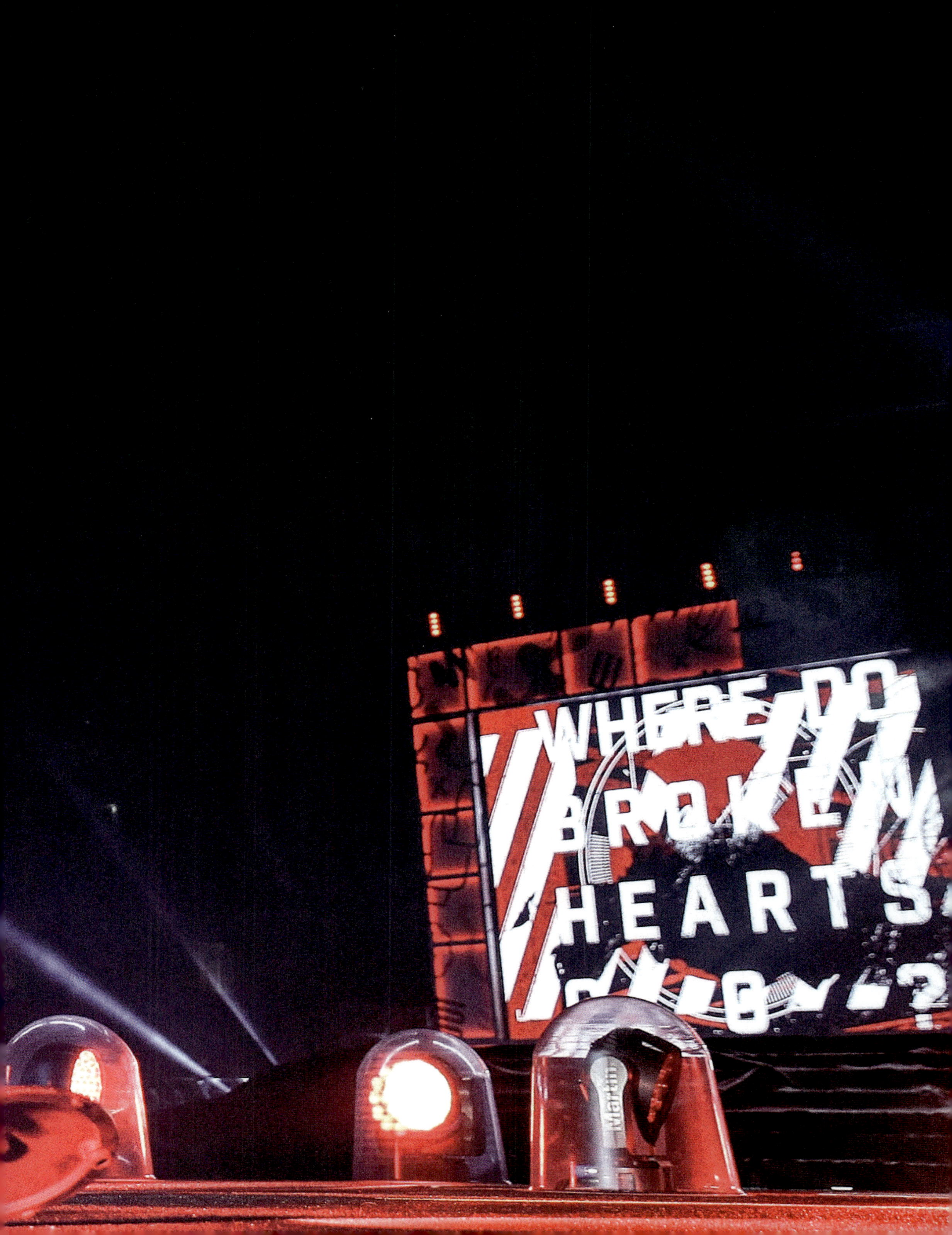
WHERE DO
HEARTS
Martin

MADE IN THE A.M.

Twelve months always elapsed between One Direction albums – every November, from 2011 through 2015, had brought one. But the November 13, 2015, release of *Made in the A.M.* had an air of finality. Zayn had left the group eight months before, and in August the rest of the band had announced they would go on hiatus from March 2016. Their fifth album was recorded knowing it would have to tide over fans until they regrouped – if they ever did. "There was definitely a vibe of making [the record] the best it can possibly be," Julian Bunetta revealed to *Billboard*. It topped charts around the world.

When 1D revealed the landing date of *Made in the A.M.*, one person didn't hesitate to share his annoyance. Justin Bieber, whose own record, *Purpose*, was also scheduled for November 13, openly claimed that they'd deliberately slotted *Made in the A.M.* into the same day as *Purpose*. Bieber's date was already known when 1D chose the same one, and he thought he knew why they'd done it.

"We're talking about them right now, so it gives them some promo, right? So that's probably why they did it," he told a New Zealand radio station, The Edge, on October 1, 2015. He suggested that it was "strategy" on their part, because who doesn't enjoy a battle of the bands? One Direction might have rued their decision to release that day: in the US, *Purpose* sold 649,000 copies, including streams, while 1D racked up a stream-inclusive 459,000. But while the band had to settle for No. 2 in the States, it was the other way round in Britain, with *Made in the A.M.* selling 93,189 copies to *Purpose*'s 90,000. And despite being released towards the end of the year, it was the UK's second-fastest-selling 2015 album, just behind Adele's *25*.

The title, *Made in the A.M.*, was coined by one of the team at their management company, Modest, and the band agreed that it suited their working style. It was a line from the song "A.M." (which, some fans suggested, stood for "After Malik" – not true), and also referred to 1D's longstanding custom of writing and recording in the small hours.

Liam said it was the band's favourite album. In a September 22, 2015, interview with Apple Music, just before they went onstage at the Apple Music Festival at London's Roundhouse, he said, "We all went off away in a different direction and wrote with a lot of different people and kind of brought it all together." Many of the standard album's 13 tracks (there are 17 on the deluxe edition) were written by one member (plus additional songwriters); five were credited to two members, generally the band's main composing duo, Liam and Louis, and none featured all five Directions. So Liam's pride in the record was understandable – they'd all gone off and done their own things, then returned with the fruits of those sessions.

Obviously, it's an album of varied styles, and a positive review in *EW* named some of the artists who might have inspired some of the songs. Praising 1D's "enormously hooky" tunes, it compared them to "musical eras more familiar to their fans' parents": the promo single "What a Feeling" conjured up Steely Dan and Fleetwood Mac; "Olivia" was a "Beatlesy ballad"; "Walking in the Wind" was reminiscent of Paul Simon's *Graceland* era.

Many reviews also noted that this was goodbye for now. In an elegant turn of phrase, *Rolling Stone*'s Rob Sheffield contended on November 13, "the kind of record the world's biggest pop group makes when it's time to say thanks for the memories."

Above: Being interviewed on ABC TV's *Good Morning America*. Rumsey Playfield, New York, August 4, 2015.

Opposite: During 1D's *Good Morning America* set at Rumsey Playfield, New York.

DRAG ME DOWN

SINGLE

RELEASED: JULY 31, 2015 (SINGLE) / NOVEMBER 13, 2015 (ALBUM)
WRITERS: JULIAN BUNETTA, JAMIE SCOTT, JOHN RYAN
PRODUCER: JULIAN BUNETTA
ALTERNATE VERSIONS: BIG PAYNO X AFTERHRS REMIX

"Bit of a surprise!" tweeted Liam at 6:12am on July 31, 2015. "Check out our new single! It's called Drag Me Down & I hope you love it as much as we do." Beneath the tweet was a link to the song on Apple Music; clicking it brought up a two-minute preview.

The next 40 minutes brought similar tweets from Harry, Louis and Niall, all of them apparently awake at an astonishingly early hour, unless they'd pre-scheduled them.

The next day, a tweet from Zayn, now five months into his solo career: "Proud of my boys the new single is sick. Big love. :) x." It was reassuring to know that there was no animosity between the two sides. Zayn was busy himself; on July 29, he'd tweeted that he had signed to RCA Records, and the day before that he joined the roster of Turn First Artists, a management company who at that time represented Ellie Goulding, Rita Ora and other big pop names. Yet the July 29 tweet was also provocatively tagged #realmusic, which could be read as a flip of the middle finger at his old band and their fans. Some Directioners tartly tweeted their feelings back at Zayn.

Anyway, "Drag Me Down" was the band's first post-Zayn single, and on its release date set a record for the most Spotify first-day streams: 4.75 million. For anyone who'd assumed that surely 1D had had their day – how many boy bands not only last long enough to make five albums but also sail along with no significant lapse in popularity? – this single proved them wrong. In its first week, when it entered the *Billboard* Hot 100 at No. 3, it was the highest-debuting song of 2015, and was downloaded 350,000 times, marking the highest introductory week of any 1D single. And this was their fifteenth – fifteenth! – single.

The band's label, Syco/Columbia, said the song "showcases a more mature One Direction sound", which it did. The Fleetwood Mac-adjacent pop-rock tune was a Bunetta/Ryan/Scott collaboration, written in March, the month Zayn departed. Because of the title, and its status as the first single made by the new fourpiece band, there was speculation that the lyrics were a message to Zayn. It was hard to understand how anyone could hear the song and come to that conclusion. A single line – just one – about offering gratitude to someone for always being there might be interpreted that way, but every other line makes it clear that it's aimed at a romantic partner, or even the perennially loyal fandom.

Opposite: Singing to 56,159 – *On the Road Again*'s second-biggest audience. MetLife Stadium, East Rutherford, New Jersey, August 5, 2015.

PERFECT

SINGLE

RELEASED: OCTOBER 16, 2015 (SINGLE) / NOVEMBER 13, 2015 (ALBUM)
WRITERS: HARRY STYLES, LOUIS TOMLINSON, JULIAN BUNETTA, JOHN RYAN, MAUREEN ANNE MCDONALD, JESSE SHATKIN, JACOB KASHER
PRODUCERS: JULIAN BUNETTA, JESSE SHATKIN, AFTERHRS
ALTERNATE VERSIONS: STRIPPED, MATOMA REMIX

***Made in the A.M.*'s second single, which was ranked No. 2 in an *Independent* countdown of all 91 of their songs – it also reached No. 2 in the UK and No. 10 in the US – excited much speculation about its subject matter.**

It was evidently a woman close to someone's heart – and since it had been written by Harry and Louis the betting was that the heart belonged to one of them.

The lyric, pored over by Directioners and an equally transfixed media, pointed to a brief but intense romance. The couple in the song had to meet in hotel rooms to avoid the paparazzi, but also took drives in the middle of the night, when they were less likely to be spotted. They enjoyed travelling – and mischief, whatever that meant. But there was also an admonition from the boyfriend; he warned the girl to avoid getting too attached because if she wanted someone she could wholeheartedly love, he wasn't the one. If this all seemed to point to one particular woman, just wait; the lyric also said – not implied, but straight-out said – that the woman had a tradition of writing songs about ex-boyfriends.

Media sites leapt on the track and came to their own conclusions. *Hollywood Life*, for one, issued a bulletin on November 11 announcing that Louis had "confirmed Taylor Swift inspired a One Direction song". Louis might have been surprised to hear that, because all he'd said (to *People* magazine the same day) was, "I think [songwriters] draw from personal experiences, so of course to a degree I'm sure that influenced some of it." That sounded like an evasion, not a confirmation.

Harry himself said something along those lines when asked by James Corden during The London Session, an Apple-sponsored performance-and-interview event held on November 14. "Everybody writes from personal experience. It's not always necessarily about what it sounds like it's about [but] sometimes it is! It's open to interpretation." Harry explained, to which Corden riposted, "Swiftly dealt with." One-upped, Harry buckled over on the sofa in a "You've got me" pose.

During a Vevo chat, Harry expanded a little more. He considered "Perfect" the album's "biggest pop song", and he wasn't wrong; it was an '80s-influenced banger, and made for dancing and swaggering. But, he said, it wasn't a "Romeo-Juliet type 'I want to be with you forever, I wanna marry you, I wanna have kids with you'," an explanation that Taylor might have found a little crushing if she watched the Vevo interview. It was, Harry said, an ode to meeting not Ms Right but Ms Right Now.

Co-writer Julian Bunetta's own view, as revealed to *Rolling Stone* on November 11? "It started as one thing and ended up where it is. Good driving song."

Opposite: This scaled-down show for the Apple Music Festival at Camden's Roundhouse, on September 22, 2015, was 1D's smallest in years.

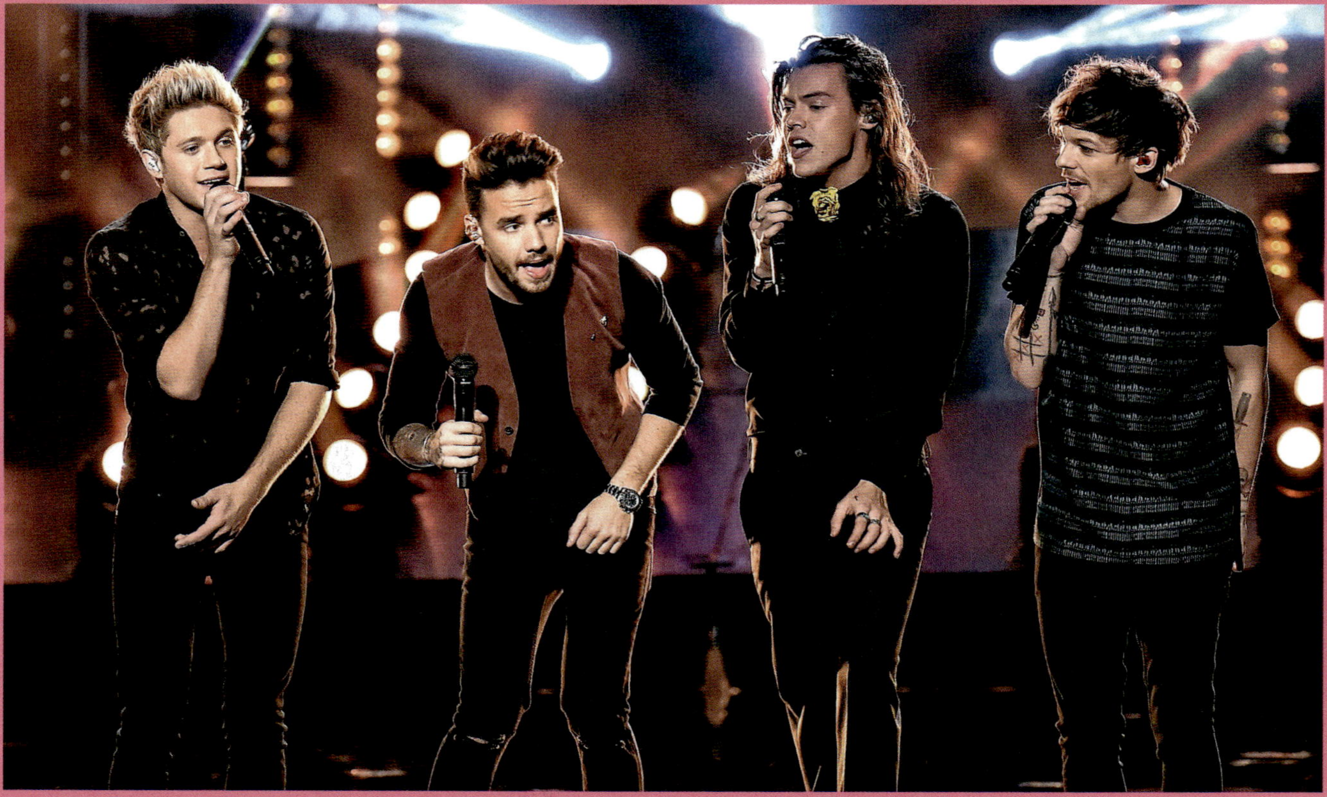

SINGLE

HISTORY

RELEASED: NOVEMBER 6, 2015 (SINGLE) / NOVEMBER 13, 2015 (ALBUM)
WRITERS: LOUIS TOMLINSON, LIAM PAYNE, JULIAN BUNETTA, JOHN RYAN, WAYNE HECTOR, ED DREWITT
PRODUCERS: JULIAN BUNETTA AND JOHN RYAN

This lilting, hand-clapping, almost-folky track is where, in effect, One Direction stopped. Despite Liam tweeting on November 26 that this single would be followed by a fourth, "Infinity" (see page 84), there were no more official singles after "History".

Obviously, neither band nor fans knew at the time that "History" was it, the single had been framed as not "goodbye", but "goodbye for now".

They intended to return after the hiatus, and that's what "History" seemed to say: that they'd been through too much together to call it quits. Each of the four remaining members had musical plans of their own, but there was no reason to think, at the November 6 release of "History", that they were considering making the split permanent. If, for no other reason, it would have been rash to abandon the safety net the group represented.

But it wasn't just the band's own past that helped to create "History". Liam explained to *EW* on November 14 that a greater part of the tune owes itself to the Directioners, "the way the fans and everyone have created this massive thing – One Direction – over the past five years". So "History", as he saw it, was closure for the fans, and "for this chapter of One Direction". ("This chapter", note: there would be another. That was the plan.)

And because the fans were uppermost in their minds during the development of "History", they invited a group of them to sing what are known as "gang vocals" or "crowd vocals" on the song. You can hear them from around 1.46 minutes, as the chorus crescendos. On the day of release, Niall tweeted about the fan choir: "Actually [Julian Bunetta] and I brought some fans to the studio to record the chorus as like a crowd vocal. So this song is really YOURS."

During a November 6 chat on the band's Vevo channel, Niall offered more insight into the song. "We chose to have 'History' on the record because we all agreed that it was one of the best songs we've had. It had that kind of '(Sittin' on) The Dock of the Bay' feel to it." He was right; in its easy rhythm was a whisper of the loose-limbed slouch that ran through "Dock of the Bay". It was, he went on, a campfire song, "easy to play, four chords". And it was aimed at everyone who had been part of their lives for the last five years, from road crew to Directioners.

The Ben Winston-directed video was also a celebration, gathering together dozens of clips of 1D playing, teasing, carousing. At the end, the four members casually wave to each other and leave the room, heading in different directions.

Opposite above: Singing in the round at *Jimmy Kimmel Live!* on November 19, 2015, in Los Angeles.

Opposite below: 1D won Artist of the Year for the second time at the American Music Awards. Los Angeles, November 22, 2015.

INFINITY

PROMOTIONAL SINGLE

RELEASED: SEPTEMBER 22, 2015 (PROMO SINGLE) / NOVEMBER 13, 2015 (ALBUM)
WRITERS: JULIAN BUNETTA, JAMIE SCOTT, JOHN RYAN
PRODUCERS: JULIAN BUNETTA AND JOHN RYAN

When, on November 26, Liam tweeted that "Infinity" would be "the next single off #MadeInTheAM" he probably wasn't expecting a response that veered from "NOOO WHY NOT WOLVES OR WHAT A FEELING" to "Liam no offense but thats the worst song on the album" to "damn typos! You spelled What A Feeling wrong".

There was the odd supportive tweet – a Directioner called Nancy replied, "Definitely – it's my favorite song from the album" – but a large number of fans wasted no time in telling Liam that One Direction had picked the wrong song to be the fourth single from *Made in the A.M.*

In the end, there was no fourth single. "Infinity" – a big, rousing guitar anthem – had already been released as a promo track, also known as an instant grat[ification] track back in September, when it came free with pre-orders of the album. Presumably, label and management decided it would be redundant to stage the marketing campaign that would be required to put it out as an official single. And "What a Feeling", the clear fan choice if there *had* been a fourth single, had already been the album's second promotional single, released a couple of weeks before Liam's tweet. (Are you keeping up?)

The intention of making "Infinity" a single had been far enough advanced that a video was filmed, with Ben Winston at the controls. In response to a fan tweet on November 13, 2020 – the fifth anniversary of *Made in the A.M.*'s release – he revealed that the video hadn't reached the final edit when it was abandoned. Somewhere, in that case, there's an unedited clip that many Directioners would give quite a bit to watch. Given the song's broodingly lovelorn lyric, it would have been interesting to see what Winston had done with it.

In a review of "Infinity" on September 23, the *NME* came straight to the point about its worth: "Basically, if 'Infinity' was strong enough to be a future single, we probably wouldn't be hearing it now." The reviewer didn't condemn it out of hand, though: "That said, this polished guitar-pop song... is no throwaway." Indeed, the "big stadium drums and ravey synth riffs" that kick in during its final minute were praised – if "Infinity" were added to the setlist of the *On the Road Again* tour, which was then approaching its end, it would sound perfect in the big rooms they were playing.

The track never made the setlist, but the audience at the first of their 25 British dates did hear a version of it. When their first show at London's O2 Arena was briefly stopped because of a tech problem, the band threw in an impromptu acoustic version of it.

Opposite: A pre-Christmas performance: the 99.7 NOW! Triple Ho Show at SAP Center. San Jose, California, December 2, 2015.

WHAT A FEELING

PROMOTIONAL SINGLE

RELEASED: NOVEMBER 11, 2015 (PROMO SINGLE) / NOVEMBER 13, 2015 (ALBUM)
WRITERS: LOUIS TOMLINSON, LIAM PAYNE, JAMIE SCOTT, DANIEL BRYER, MIKE NEEDLE
PRODUCER: JAMIE SCOTT

This was the song that Directioners *really* wanted – judging by their tweets – as *Made in the A.M.*'s fourth single.

They were in good company, because Louis also loved it, as did Liam – tweeting a link to "What a Feeling" on November 11, Louis said, "Really love this one. Payno, this one is your fav right?" It should have been a Payno favourite, because it was one of the four songs he and Louis wrote together for the standard album.

During the track-by-track discussion posted on Vevo on November 25 [the band's Vevo chat was divided into three parts and made available on different dates in November], Louis said it was one of his favourites from the album because it offered a different flavour and tone from the other 12 tracks. "It's got a little Fleetwood [Mac] influence in there," he said, and he was right.

There was more than a little Fleetwood influence; without explicitly copying any Mac track, the band and producer Jamie Scott managed to perfectly capture their mid-'70s California airiness. As *Spin* wrote on the day it came out, "Seriously, those floaty oohs and aahs are right out Stevie Nicks and co.'s playbook." Louis singled it out as the song that would sound perfect "with your roof down in your car, feeling like a little bit of a chief". Certainly, more than anything else on the record, "What a Feeling" demanded to be heard while driving, preferably with the wind in your hair. And the other Fleetwoodesque element was a melancholy lyric, about a girl who was passionately loved by the guy, and seemed to return his feelings, but was frustratingly out of reach much of the time.

(Those following the Bieber/1D spat ignited by Bieber when he learned that his *Purpose* and 1D's *Made in the A.M.* were coming out on the same day might have noticed that on November 9 – just three days before "What a Feeling" was made available – he debuted a track called "The Feeling". Coincidence? More than likely.)

Julian Bunetta, who wasn't involved in the writing of "What a Feeling", admitted to feeling "so pissed off" when Jamie Scott played it for him. "I was so mad... so pissed off, because the chorus was so good," he told *Rolling Stone* on November 11. "I was just jealous." But no hard feelings: he subsequently spent many a night dancing to it at home.

The song achieved a second life on October 4, 2020, when Directioners launched a campaign to get it to No. 1. Enough people complied with the hashtag #StreamWhatAFeeling for it to get into the US and UK iTunes charts, though it didn't quite top the charts.

Opposite above: At 102.7 KIIS FM's Jingle Ball 2015. Staples Center, Los Angeles, December 4, 2015.

Opposite below: Ringing in 2016 the American way at Dick Clark's New Year's Rockin' Eve with Ryan Seacrest. Los Angeles, December 31, 2015.

Overleaf: At 106.1 KISS FM's Jingle Ball 2015. American Airlines Center. Dallas, Texas, December 1, 2015.

billboard
HOLLYWOOD
PARTY
WITH
RYAN SEACREST
ROCKIN'
'16
DICK CLARK'S

DICK CLARK'S
NEW YEAR'S
ROCKIN'
EVE '16
RYAN SEACREST

OTHER SONGS

There are more than enough 1D unreleased demos, cover versions, rarities and unclassifiable outliers – such as an August 2015 performance at Radio 1's Live Lounge in which they covered Rihanna's "FourFiveSeconds" and Natalie Imbruglia's "Torn" – to fill a dozen albums. On the last two 1D LPs, for example, Liam was learning the art of remixing and production, and his Big Payno tracks were starting to pop up.

On the *Perfect* EP (downloadable from October 21, 2015), he produced a remix of "Drag Me Down", with rapper LunchMoney Lewis on the mic, while a Payno reworking of "You & I" was available on the bundled release of that *Midnight Memories* single.

Then there were the cover versions, of which the most well-known was "One Way or Another"/"Teenage Kicks", their mash-up of the '70s Blondie and Undertones hits. It was a chart-topper in 2013, with the proceeds donated to the UK charity fundraiser, Red Nose Day. "Teenage Kicks" was an apt choice for a band who were mostly still in their teens, and they gave it some high-spirited gusto. There was also a charity release of David Bowie's imperishable "Heroes" in aid of Help for Heroes, a charity supporting UK military veterans. It was dramatically sung by the last 16 finalists on *The X Factor*, then released as a single on November 19, 2010.

But there were also plenty of other covers, from the *X Factor* days onward. Harry's audition song was Stevie Wonder's "Isn't She Lovely", performed a cappella – quite a feat because of the high notes. It's worth finding the performance online just to see Harry's cherubic face wreathed in smiles when Simon Cowell waves him through to the next round. Liam's bravura "Cry Me a River" – the Justin Bieber hit – is also very watchable, especially for the moment when he doubles over in joy as he too goes through.

Then there are all the covers they performed as a group on the show, from Coldplay's "Viva la Vida" early in the series to the emotional take on Imbruglia's "Torn" in the final. But that wasn't the last time they sang other artists' hits. Throughout their touring career the band put their stamp on a wide and unpredictable selection. "Valerie" (The Zutons) made it into the *Up All Night* tour, they broke out Dolly Parton's "9 to 5" when they played Nashville on 2014's *Where We Are* tour, and Abba's "Mamma Mia" in Stockholm on the same jaunt.

A link-up with US chain store Target yielded a limited-edition version of *Take Me Home* with five exclusive-to-Target extra songs: "Magic", "Truly, Madly, Deeply", "Irresistible", "One Thing (Live)" and "I Wish (Live)". The last two were recorded during shows on the *Up All Night* tour. And copies of another Target special release, the *Made in the A.M.* album with four different covers, each featuring a band member, are often available on eBay, with a significant markup on price.

But the most-desired 1D rarities, according to many Directioners, are unreleased demos. Interviewed on the *Audacy Check In* podcast on October 8, 2025, Louis estimated that up to 60 exist. "I don't think [they'll ever come out]. I'm kind of funny about that, especially when they leak, because there's a reason they've not made the record." Some can be found online, such as the upbeat, folk-poppy "She Got Away" (recorded for *Four* and leaked in 2023) and "Pick Your Poison", an amiable arena-rocker that didn't make the cut on *Made in the A.M.*

Maybe what's needed is one more 1D album, this one celebrating the rarities, the B-sides and the ones-that-got-away...

Opposite: And ...scream! Dick Clark's New Year's Rockin' Eve with Ryan Seacrest. Los Angeles, December 31, 2015.

PART 2

HARRY STYLES.

HARRY STYLES

Harry Styles, released May 12, 2017, was a definitive line in the sand between Styles' past and his future. Behind him: One Direction and a life in which musical choices were made for him, not by him. Ahead: having the final say about what he recorded, and the joy, as he told *Rolling Stone* on April 18, 2017, of having "time to live with a song... it's heaven." His debut allowed him to finally write about his real life – things he'd actually experienced, rather than fictional "stories". More than anything, he wanted to be honest – and it got him a global No. 1 record.

MEET ME IN THE HALLWAY

ALBUM TRACK

RELEASED: MAY 12, 2017
WRITERS: HARRY STYLES, TYLER JOHNSON, MITCH ROWLAND, JEFF BHASKER, ALEX SALIBIAN, RYAN NASCI
PRODUCERS: TYLER JOHNSON, JEFF BHASKER, ALEX SALIBIAN
ALTERNATE VERSION: *BEHIND THE ALBUM*

As an album opener, Styles could hardly have chosen a more startling one. "Meet Me in the Hallway" takes any expectations a listener might have and bins them. "I'm a pretty private person," he said during an interview with Canadian news programme *Etalk* on December 9, 2017. "Some of the stuff on the album I would never choose to talk about [but] when you're writing it's therapeutic to get it out and be vulnerable in that way."

He wanted to emulate the kind of music he himself connected with, and the quality that he most admired in others' music – honesty.

Well.

The album's overarching theme seems to be a relationship with a woman that was either on–off or had just ended for good. He's never said who she was – among fans and media, Kendall Jenner's name often cropped up – but whatever happened, it left its mark. In the first verse of this dreamy, near-psychedelic tune, she's in her bedroom and he's hovering down the hall; he's said goodbye and is agonizing over whether the relationship can be saved.

Whatever has happened is due to his own failings, he admits, and tells himself it's up to him to change. There's a fogginess to his voice, and an echoing dreaminess that makes him sound as if he's communicating from a very long way away. (He's playing an electronic instrument called an Omnichord on the song, which may have produced the arpeggiated harp sound in the opening bars.)

The most striking line here – still in the first verse – is the penultimate one, shortly before the chorus. He's in such emotional pain that he wants morphine. That's not a word that ever cropped up in a One Direction song – it's more usually found in tracks like the Rolling Stones' "Sister Morphine".
And it's made all the more potent by the music: the downbeat guitar chords that open the song evoke two Pink Floyd songs, both from *The Dark Side of the Moon*: "The Great Gig in the Sky" and "Breathe (In the Air"), tracks that were similarly brooding. (N.B. Styles is such a Floyd fan that he had their 13-minute "Shine on You Crazy Diamond" serve as the intro music on one of his tours.)

The melancholy is replicated on the next track, "Sign of the Times", but feels more painful here because, as the opening track, it hits harder. His misery and regret is thrust upon us without warning.

So how did the relationship pan out?

Fairly harmoniously, going by an April 8, 2017, *Rolling Stone* interview: "Sometimes you want to tip the hat, and sometimes you just want to give them the whole cap", he said, looking back at it with what sounded like fondness.

Opposite above: "I can't hear you!" *Today* show. Rockefeller Plaza, New York, May 9, 2017.

Opposite below: Opening night of Harry's first solo run, *Live on Tour*. Masonic SF Auditorium, San Francisco, September 19, 2017.

citi
CONCERT
SERIES ON
TODAY

SIGN OF THE TIMES

SINGLE

RELEASED: APRIL 7, 2017 (SINGLE) / MAY 12, 2017 (ALBUM)
WRITERS: HARRY STYLES, TYLER JOHNSON, MITCH ROWLAND, JEFF BHASKER, ALEX SALIBIAN, RYAN NASCI
PRODUCER: JEFF BHASKER
ALTERNATE VERSION: *BEHIND THE ALBUM*

This track was, as Styles said in a 2017 documentary, *Harry Styles: Behind the Album*, the song that made the album "feel like it was starting to be an album. I finished lunch early and sat at the piano for five minutes".

It came together faster than any of the record's other songs, and "became a bridge into trying a bunch of different stuff". Adding a gospel choir was one of them, and as he watched them record, he felt "emotional". He hadn't expected to feel overcome with pride and gratitude, but there it was: he'd written a song, and now 26 gospel singers were turning it into a unique track: "It felt like it was growing into its own thing. It was pretty amazing."

Styles had several potential album titles in mind, including *Pink* – he was impressed by Clash bassist Paul Simonon having called it "the only true rock'n'roll colour". He eventually dismissed *Pink* from the running, though he did adopt the colour for this single's artwork. On the sleeve he appears as a murky silhouette, waist-deep in water, facing away from the camera. All around is an apocalyptic pink-red sky, and he appears to be facing a submerged body whose hands and feet are just visible.

After deciding the debut wouldn't be called *Pink*, he wanted *Sign of the Times*. The album's co-writer and co-producer Jeff Bhasker, dissuaded him: "I don't know. I mean, it's been used," he said, according to *Rolling Stone*'s April 2017 interview. Quite: who needed comparisons to Prince's venerated 1987 album *Sign o' the Times*?

So *Harry Styles* it was, but the generic name was offset by this sprawling cut – 5.40 mins, which is endless for a pop single. It started life as a voicenote on Harry's phone; later, while recording at Geejam Studios in Portland, Jamaica, in the autumn of 2016, he was playing it on the piano, doodling around with what he and his collaborators had come up with. "We fleshed it out a little bit. Then he jumped on the mic, I played piano and we cut that whole record in three hours," Bhasker told the *Hits* music-industry site on May 30, 2017. The amazing thing, he added, was that Rob Stringer, then CEO of Styles' label, Columbia, didn't request a radio edit – Stringer felt it should be sent to radio just as it was: long and melancholy, yet soaring. The lyric, Styles told *Rolling Stone*, was about a woman in childbirth; the baby is born healthy, yet the mother doesn't survive. The sobering subject was offset by a chorus so catchy that the song hit No. 1 in Australia and the UK, and No. 4 in the US.

Opposite: Engrossed in the music at a show for SiriusXM from West Hollywood's Roxy Theatre, May 17, 2017.

DUNKIRK
IMAX
PREMIERE
DUNKIRK

CAROLINA

ALBUM TRACK

RELEASED: MAY 12, 2017
WRITERS: HARRY STYLES, TYLER JOHNSON, MITCH ROWLAND, JEFF BHASKER, ALEX SALIBIAN, RYAN NASCI, THOMAS HULL
PRODUCERS: TYLER JOHNSON, JEFF BHASKER, ALEX SALIBIAN, KID HARPOON
ALTERNATE VERSION: *BEHIND THE ALBUM*

Coming straight after the downtempo, reflective "Sign of the Times", "Carolina" is a jaunty, upbeat change of pace that keeps the album fresh. It also revived Styles himself at a time when the recording process was nagging at him, prompting a cycle of worry.

Harry, Bhasker and the other collaborators had written nearly every song for the album, but needed one more, and they couldn't seem to move things along.

They'd had "a week, two weeks, of being in a real funk," Styles told Radio 1's Nick Grimshaw on May 12, 2017 – the LP's release day. "Everything was terrible." He was beginning to have doubts about whether the record was on the right path.

Then he met the woman who restored his confidence. Her name was Townes; (South) Carolina was her home state. They met on a blind date – apparently, even Harry Styles goes on blind dates – arranged by her sister, Gilland Jones, an actress who'd appeared in several Disney Channel series. Townes was then a 20-year-old attending UCLA (University of California, Los Angeles), majoring in French and philosophy – there's a reference in the lyric to her proclivity for books.

Though there was only that single date, it made enough of an impression that Harry got a song out of it. It turned out to be exactly what *Harry Styles* needed. It was his first date in a while; in fact, it seemed to be his first social event in some time, which explains the impact it had. He'd faced day after day of fruitless studio grind, and suddenly he was out on the town, enjoying his connection – even if it was short-lived – with a smart, attractive woman. That night, he said on *Behind the Album*, had been "the first time in a long time I'd been out and done something and then came back to the studio and decided to write about that."

Styles had always been a private individual, and that extended to talking about girlfriends – when asked whether his songs are about them, he generally resorted to the bland catch-all, "You're influenced by your experiences." Not this time. Not only did he tell Grimshaw it was about a specific person – her name actually appeared in the lyrics! – he revealed that she'd found out about it because her dad saw him premiering the track on America's *Today* show a few days earlier, and sent his daughter a voicenote saying, "I think he just sang a song about you on the TV."

"You can feel a waft of relaxed Jamaican island life immediately," wrote a *Variety* critic on the LP's release day. That turned out to be what *Harry Styles* had been missing – that little bit of fun.

Opposite above: A scene from Harry's first movie role, *Dunkirk*, released around the time of his debut album – 2017 was a busy year.
Opposite below: Arriving at the Odeon Leicester Square, London, for *Dunkirk*'s world premiere. July 13, 2017.

TWO GHOSTS

SINGLE

RELEASED: AUGUST 20, 2017 (SINGLE) / MAY 12, 2017 (ALBUM)
WRITERS: HARRY STYLES, MITCH ROWLAND, TYLER JOHNSON, JOHN RYAN, JULIAN BUNETTA
PRODUCERS: TYLER JOHNSON, JEFF BHASKER, ALEX SALIBIAN
ALTERNATE VERSION: *BEHIND THE ALBUM*, RECORDED AT METROPOLIS STUDIOS, LONDON (SPOTIFY SINGLES)

"You're going to be asked about this. I'm doing you a favour here," Styles was informed by Radio 1's Nick Grimshaw during the *Harry Styles* release-day interview.

"This" was "Two Ghosts", the album's second single, and its most guessed-about track. That was because its lyrics were seen in a trailer for *Behind the Album*, and when the fandom got their teeth into a lyric, they picked it apart. "Two Ghosts" got a thorough going-over online, and the question Directioners wanted answered was: Who was he singing about?

Many were positive that the muse behind this rootsy, alt-country ballad was Taylor Swift. Many were positive that it wasn't. The evidence in favour was a physical description that included red lipstick – Swift had made a trademark of wearing it – and blue eyes. The evidence against was tattoos – the subject of the song not only had them, she'd acquired more since Harry had last seen her. Swift had made her feelings plain about tattoos as far back as October 2012, when she told *Taste of Country*, "I don't think I could ever commit [to permanently inking her body]." But if not Taylor, then who?

That was why Grimshaw stepped in and asked the question. He was almost compelled to, because speculation had become so clamorous that the possible Swift link was covered on Radio 1's *Newsbeat*. When Grimshaw told him he was doing Harry a favour by addressing it, Styles muttered, "Weird favour." Then, reluctantly: "I think it's pretty self-explanatory." Eventually, he settled on a roundabout explanation, saying that in any relationship, things changed and eventually the two parties no longer felt the same.

The origin story of "Two Ghosts" contains a real surprise: it was written for One Direction. He and co-writers Julian Bunetta and John Ryan intended the track to appear on *Made in the A.M.* But, he told *Rolling Stone* in 2019 during the *Fine Line* promo campaign, he changed his mind: "The story was just a bit too personal." At that point, in 2015, he was just beginning to explore the idea of writing about things he hadn't felt comfortable tackling earlier in 1D's career. "I just became aware of a piece of me going, 'I want to sing the whole thing,'" and that couldn't happen in the band. He once ruefully called One Direction a "democracy", because no one member would be allowed to solo on an entire song.

He revived the track for *Harry Styles*, and as he worked with Bhasker and the musicians Bhasker had put together for the album project, it became the song he'd envisaged all along. Its relatively weak chart performance – No. 58 in the UK and No. 18 on the US Bubbling Under the Hot 100 chart – is a mystery.

Opposite: Putting his stamp on New York's much-loved Radio City Music Hall, September 28, 2017.

SWEET CREATURE

ALBUM TRACK

RELEASED: MAY 12, 2017
WRITERS: HARRY STYLES AND THOMAS HULL
PRODUCERS: TYLER JOHNSON, JEFF BHASKER, ALEX SALIBIAN, KID HARPOON
ALTERNATE VERSION: *BEHIND THE ALBUM*

The debut album produced only one promo single, and this was it – a deeply felt acoustic ballad that had been the first track composed for the record.

On May 2, Harry announced its release via Twitter: "Sweet Creature is available now. Album is available in ten days. I am available always." That last sentence might have had something to do with the tweet getting close to 300,000 likes.

He threw his entire self into the recording of this song, exerting the whole power of his voice. It's more demanding to control and modulate a voice on a quiet song than it is on a full-scale rocker, and "Sweet Creature" was a test of his ability, which he passed. He also performed the song at Abbey Road Studios for *Behind the Album*, and that performance showed what he could really do as a vocalist. Within the confines of this delicate, loving tribute to an unidentified someone – clearly someone very dear; the gist was that being with her felt like coming home – he soared and swooped, yet never spilled over into exaggerated pathos. Watching the footage in the control room afterwards, Jeff Bhasker erupted with admiration. "Hallelujah! Hallelujah! Harry, you're *so good*! Praise Jesus! Hal-ay-loo-ya!" Styles took the praise as any English person would: he emitted a self-conscious "hnnh".

He wrote the song with producer/musician Tom "Kid Harpoon" Hull at his Los Angeles studio, Harpoon's Barn. It was the first time they'd worked together; the partnership proved so productive that Harpoon was promoted to major collaborator, writing and producing large swathes of Styles's next three albums. In 2023, Styles won Grammys for Album of the Year and Pop Vocal Album of the Year.

As ever, the media's desire to know who the song was about was matched by Harry's desire not to say. Styles admitted that it was about a specific person, but when pressed during an interview with American radio presenter Zach Sang on May 4, he retreated to his usual opaque position.

"I think most songs are written for one listener... It's so much easier to say something in a song than it is to say it to someone." He appreciated a song's capacity to allow feelings to be shared in a way that would have felt awkward if he'd simply come out and said it. "[I like] being able to wrap up everything that you want to say in three and a half minutes and say it in a song." One theory was that the subject was his sister, Gemma, who represented "home" for Harry.

Reviews were mainly warm; *Spin* summed things up with the headline, "If You Didn't Already Think Harry Styles Is Serious, His New Song 'Sweet Creature' Might Sway You."

Opposite: Giving his all at the ARIA Awards at the Star Casino, Sydney, in November 28, 2017.

ONLY ANGEL

RELEASED: MAY 12, 2017
WRITERS: HARRY STYLES, TYLER JOHNSON, MITCH ROWLAND, JEFF BHASKER, ALEX SALIBIAN, RYAN NASCI
PRODUCERS: TYLER JOHNSON, JEFF BHASKER, ALEX SALIBIAN
ALTERNATE VERSION: *BEHIND THE ALBUM*

In which Styles gives voice to his inner rock beast, and then some. "Only Angel" probably didn't have Metallica looking over their shoulders, but it's undoubtedly Styles as we've rarely heard him – openly carnal and howling at the moon.

Classic rocker Paul Rodgers comes to mind here; though the vocal on "Only Angel" has been likened to Mick Jagger, this rough-edged performance is closer to the kind of thing Rodgers was doing with Bad Company in the '70s. (He's a fellow Northerner, too.)

Apart from its muted piano-and-choir introduction, it's a vivid contrast to virtually everything else on the record – right here, at its halfway point, the slightly-psychedelic-slightly-folky-slightly-rootsy atmosphere gets distinctly... explicit.

Styles wrote and recorded it at his place in London, he told Nick Grimshaw during their Radio 1 interview on the album's release day. He got it done in one take, and it has the rough-and-ready quality of a song that hasn't been tinkered with – one and done, that's it. He called the track "perky" – a kind of aw-shucks way of acknowledging that it's a bit of a bruiser. He listened to it again the night before the interview, just to see how it felt: "I went for a walk, it hit midnight and it was raining. It was a very emotional experience."

The question of who it might be about seems more urgent than usual here. The song is so libidinous that his usual "It could be anyone" response wouldn't cut the mustard. The lyric refers to the finger he broke and the knuckles he grazed as he crossed the bedroom floor on hands and knees, about her skirt being so revealing he couldn't introduce her to his mother, about her skill in bed. The storyline has more in common with Rick James' "Super Freak" than anything Harry had done before.

The song certainly unleashed something in him. A review in *Transistor* on May 17 noted the difference between "the usually humble Styles" and the man he is on "Only Angel", "exud[ing] arrogance when almost bragging about the girl who was the muse for this track", while *Variety*'s release-day review said he owed a fair bit "to a certain Rolling Stone, he wears the soul claps and 'woo-hoos' of 'Only Angel' as though he's the lost child of Jagger himself". *Slate*, however, accused him of "drag[ging along] the Stones' scraggly trail of misogyny... 'Only Angel' is directed at a stereotypical lust object lacking in distinguishing traits".

Those who had a guess about the "angel" pointed to sometime-girlfriend Kendall Jenner. Their relationship ebbed and flowed as they split and got back together, but the "Gotcha" evidence: she was a Victoria's Secret "angel", complete with wings, at the chain's 2015 fashion show.

Opposite: Giving his all at the ARIA Awards at the Star Casino, Sydney, in November 28, 2017.

KIWI

SINGLE

RELEASED: OCTOBER 21, 2017 (SINGLE) / MAY 12, 2017 (ALBUM)
WRITERS: HARRY STYLES, TYLER JOHNSON, JEFF BHASKER, MITCH ROWLAND, ALEX SALIBIAN, RYAN NASCI
PRODUCERS: TYLER JOHNSON, JEFF BHASKER, ALEX SALIBIAN
ALTERNATE VERSION: *BEHIND THE ALBUM*

As uncharacteristic as "Only Angel" was, it was just an amuse-bouche for the sex-drugs-rock'n'roll-and-pregnancy of "Kiwi", *Harry Styles*' third and final single.

While *Slate* reviewer Carl Wilson was generally unmoved by most of the album, he did find that "only... 'Kiwi', a little battle-of-the-sexes/fame-monster playlet, skirts any genuine eroticism".

That's not bad for a track Styles considered "a joke" at first. "I was getting out a lot of energy," he explained on Radio 1. "I hadn't written in a long time and this is what came out of it." It gradually became one of his favourite songs.

He intended to change the name, but never got around to it, inadvertently creating a rod for his own back. Fans turned up at shows armed with kiwi fruits, which they lobbed onto the stage as a gesture of love. Harry slipped on one in the middle of a set at London's Hammersmith Apollo on October 30, 2017, though he managed to stay on his feet. "There was an actual kiwi onstage and that was the culprit," he informed the crowd. "There was a green, seedy mush on the floor. Oh, there's another one. If anyone else brought fruit to this show... did anyone else? Shame on you."

He had a gig coming up at the O2 Apollo in Manchester three days after the Hammersmith incident, and the Asda Superstore in Hulme decided to "protect a fellow Mancunian" by banning the sale of kiwis to under-25s, a spokesperson told the *Mirror*.

"Kiwi" was the equivalent of an energy drink: 2.56 minutes of high-voltage, guitar-based swagger, fronted by a Styles who sounded like he'd been doing this all his life. He sang it like a rock star. Lyrically, it took on a female archetype as old as rock'n'roll itself: the smoking, drinking, drugging bad girl who lives her life exactly as she chooses. When she gets pregnant, she lets him know, but then crushingly adds that she has no further use for him. That's the actual chorus: her announcement that he's going to be a father. Stirring (and catchy) stuff – and kiwis aren't mentioned.

Likewise, no kiwis were involved in the video, helmed by directing duo Us (Christopher Barrett and Luke Taylor) and shot in a single day. Rather, it follows a group of young children through a school and culminates in a food fight – and then a herd of puppies arrive and made short work of the leftover cupcakes. "It was a lot of messy fun," Taylor told *GQ* in 2020. "And I'd argue you couldn't find a nicer pop star than Harry." Though it only charted at No. 66 in the UK, it eventually went platinum there and in America.

Opposite above & below: With honoree Lindsey Buckingham of Fleetwood Mac at MusiCares Person of the Year ceremony. Radio City, New York, January 26, 2018.

Overleaf: Accompanied, as he often is onstage, by the LGBTQ flag. AccorHotels Arena, Paris, March 13, 2018.

OOD MAC

EVER SINCE NEW YORK

ALBUM TRACK

RELEASED: MAY 12, 2017
WRITERS: HARRY STYLES, TYLER JOHNSON, JEFF BHASKER, MITCH ROWLAND, ALEX SALIBIAN, RYAN NASCI
PRODUCERS: TYLER JOHNSON, JEFF BHASKER, ALEX SALIBIAN
ALTERNATE VERSION: *BEHIND THE ALBUM*

Because Taylor Swift had an apartment in New York, conclusions were jumped to when this track's name was announced. "Speculation has erupted on social media around the title and its similarities with a Taylor Swift track titled 'Welcome To New York'," reported *Sky News* on April 14.

That speculation was a considerable leap of faith, as neither the song nor the lyric had been released, and until he debuted the track on *Saturday Night Live* on April 15, there was no way of knowing what it was about.

There was also an inconvenient question of timing. Taylor bought her place in 2014, but their brief romance took place between December 2012 and January 2013. While they were photographed in New York's Central Park then, she was only in the city to see One Direction's Madison Square Garden show.

Swift, it's now generally accepted, had nothing to do with a song described by *Rolling Stone* in an April 2017 interview, as "a desperate meditation on loss and longing". It seems far more likely that it relates to his stepfather Robin Twist's struggle with cancer. Fans have suggested that it was at Memorial Sloan Kettering Cancer Center in New York that he received the news that his illness was terminal; he passed away in June 2017. The song mentions Brooklyn, where, to extrapolate from the lyric, it seems Harry learned about the diagnosis, and the second verse emphasizes that Harry, who had never been prayerful, has been praying hard "ever since New York".

More was revealed at a secret four-song show he staged on May 10, 2017, for iHeart Radio. His first ever solo gig, it took place in the Rough Trade record shop, which happened to be in Brooklyn. He began with "Ever Since New York", which was followed by "Sign of the Times", "Two Ghosts", "Carolina" and, to finish, another go-round for "Ever Since New York". Twice in one mini-show? That spoke volumes about the track's importance to him. He told the small crowd that the song was about an experience at a hotel near the venue – later identified by someone at the show as the McCarren.

Two years later, during a November 2019 interview with Apple Music's Zane Lowe, Harry discussed the pressure he piled on himself while making his second album, *Fine Line*. He felt he had to pack *Fine Line* full of big songs, because "the last record [*Harry Styles*] wasn't a radio record". He might just as well have pointed a finger at "Ever Since New York", which was beautiful and sad, but in no way a "big song".

Opposite: Another view of Styles' show at AccorHotels Arena, Paris, on March 13, 2018.

WOMAN

RELEASED: MAY 12, 2017
WRITERS: HARRY STYLES, TYLER JOHNSON, JEFF BHASKER, MITCH ROWLAND, ALEX SALIBIAN, RYAN NASCI
PRODUCERS: TYLER JOHNSON, JEFF BHASKER, ALEX SALIBIAN
ALTERNATE VERSION: *BEHIND THE ALBUM*

In a May 17 review, Emma Garland of *Vice* felt that this slow, hip-grinding admission of jealousy was based on Elton John's "Bennie and the Jets". She was referring to the staccato guitar stabs at the start, which led into a menacing glam-rock stomp through the rest of the track.

"This is literally 'Bennie and the Jets'," she wrote. "And if you think putting an inexplicable honking duck noise all over it will distract from that then you are absolutely right."

That duck, which honked every few seconds, was Styles. For reasons unexplained, he made a quacking noise while recording, and producers Jeff Bhasker, Tyler Johnson and Alex Salibian added studio trickery that made him sound more like a duck. He told Nick Grimshaw on April 7, 2017, that when his family heard it, his stepdad brought him back down to earth.

"I played [the album] to them the first time and there's one song on the album where there's a bit with a vocal effect on it. The whole album finished, then my stepdad said, 'I've one question. Where did you get the duck from – how did you get a duck in the studio?' I was, like, 'That was me, thanks'." The *Bustle* site mused, "The duck sound really is making the entire album. Styles will forever be associated with a duck now." That prediction turned out not to be true – probably to his relief.

The BBC website claimed on May 12 that the track "was inspired after the writing sessions for the album were finished for the day. How meta." At least, the spoken-word phrase that opens the track was. The American-accented voice belonging to Salibian – he's also a guitarist, keyboardist and musical director of Styles' live band – wonders whether they should check what rom-coms they could find on Netflix that night. Then – bang, Salibian adds a piano glissando, the guitar stabs kick in and "Woman" sinuously uncoils. (This moment can be seen in Styles' Abbey Road in-studio performance, which was included in the May 15 *Behind the Album* documentary.)

"When I was [recording] in Jamaica, we got into a routine where we'd write, have dinner and then watch countless romantic comedies, mindless movies, anything Nicholas Sparks has ever done," Styles told Grimshaw. "There was a lot of that – I always circle back to *The Notebook*." His admiration of Sparks' rom-dram novels could well explain his propensity for romantically fraught songs.

Like, say, "Woman". The intense jealousy it encapsulates – he can't stand to think of his ex with her new man, demanding that she understand how broken he is – could be a plot for a film. He's never revealed her identity.

Opposite: Solo headlining New York's Madison Square Garden for the first time. June 21, 2018.

FROM THE DINING TABLE

ALBUM TRACK

RELEASED: MAY 12, 2017
WRITERS: HARRY STYLES, TYLER JOHNSON, JEFF BHASKER, MITCH ROWLAND, ALEX SALIBIAN, RYAN NASCI
PRODUCERS: TYLER JOHNSON, JEFF BHASKER, ALEX SALIBIAN
ALTERNATE VERSION: *BEHIND THE ALBUM*

As *Harry Styles* opened with a ballad full of heartache, so it ended with one. During a Q&A at the GRAMMY Museum in Los Angeles on September 15, Harry identified the melancholy "From the Dining Table" as "the one that makes me feel the most."

"It's the most different than what I expected myself to write and it's probably the most honest that I've been in a song as well. It's the most personal to me, and I think my favourite one."

Bhasker, there with him, emphasized their "authentic and viscerally honest" approach to not just the song but the whole album – yet this closing track is by a long way the most unguarded, and the most raw. Styles could hardly have been more open: it's about self-love of the physical kind.

It's in the second line: awakening in a hotel, he feels lonely, pleasures himself, goes back to sleep and when he wakes later, sometime before midday, drinks until he's drunk. He feels miserable. And then, we're led to believe, he sits down and writes this song, listing the ways in which he misses his ex. Her departure is the reason he's alone in a hotel bed.

This is the side of pop stardom that outsiders don't see – the unglamorous loneliness of being in a luxurious hotel with only yourself for company. His girl went some time ago, after an argument, and now has someone new, while he's drowning in silence. Worst of all, the ex seems to be just fine – she's even given the new boyfriend a T-shirt of Harry's. This is a slow, bluesy number primarily comprised of Mitch Rowland's guitar work and Styles using a close-mic technique, leaning right into it and murmuring.

Discussing it with *Rolling Stone* two years later, he had mixed emotions, even some regret, about allowing such a raw insight into his life. "I thought I was being *so* honest, just because there's one line about having a wank," he said on December 13, 2019 – the release date of his second album, *Fine Line* (and, by chance, Taylor Swift's 30th birthday). "I had no idea. You write a song that's pretty open and honest, and you think, 'That's just *my* song,' but then you hand it over to people, and it's like, 'Oh f***!'" While writing and recording, he hadn't even thought of it as a "song". He considers songs to be "just voicenotes" until they're heard by the public.

And yet... to some reviewers, it was one of the best *Harry Styles* songs. In an album review on May 19, 2017, *Atwood* magazine singles it out as "perhaps the only believable track on the album in terms of emotional experience and originality."

Opposite: Glittering at the Xcel Energy Center, Saint Paul, Minnesota, on July 1, 2018.
Overleaf: The first of two dates at New York's Madison Square Garden. June 21, 2018.

BLACK LIVES MATTER
BLACK LIVES MATTER
BLACK LIVES MATTER
BLACK LIVES MATTER

CHASING THE MUSE

Tracking Harry's love life has kept the internet busy for years, interest fuelled by his habit of including vague – and not-so-vague – references to his romantic partners in his songs. Single life might have its delights, but he hasn't spent much time exploring them; in the 16 years since joining One Direction, he's almost always been spoken for. Even before 1D, he was in a relationship, albeit a longish-distance one, as the 76 miles between Holmes Chapel and Solihull – home of his first girlfriend, Felicity Skinner – meant that he and Felicity couldn't see each other as often as they'd have liked.

They met through a Holmes Chapel friend in 2009, when both were 15, and spent nearly a year together. Felicity categorized their relationship as puppy love – he was "very romantic and, yes, shy", she told the *Sunday People* in April 2012. They drifted apart as a couple, but they kept in touch until shortly before the Judges' Houses segment of *The X Factor*, after which they lost contact.

His next romance, for a few months in 2011, was with Caroline Flack, who was then hosting *The Xtra Factor*. She was 14 years his senior, which was part of her appeal: "He joked about being attracted to older women," she wrote in her memoir, *Storm in a C Cup*. She said things went swimmingly until he was seen coming out of her house one morning. "And once that was out, it was open season. After that anyone could say anything [about the age gap]."

Another short relationship, with *Inbetweeners* actress Emily Atack, followed in May 2012. "Harry and I had a laugh," she told *Reveal* in August 2013. "It was brief, but fun, and then we moved on." That meant that when he ran into Taylor Swift a few months later – he'd first met her at the Kids' Choice Awards in March 2012 – he was available. And, having recently split with Kennedy family scion Conor Kennedy, so was she. Again, they weren't together long, but it was long enough to (supposedly) inspire a couple of Swift songs, "Style" and "Out of the Woods". The Styles' song "Two Ghosts" is said to be about Swift, though he's never confirmed it.

Harry and Kendall Jenner were the definition of an "on-off relationship" for about four years, starting in early 2014, and surviving through several breakups and makeups until around 2017. During their "on" periods, the underprivileged pair holidayed in St Barts and skied in Mammoth Mountain, California.

His next substantive relationship, from summer 2017 to July 2018, was with French model Camille Rowe. Hers was the voice heard at the end of "Cherry", talking to a friend on the phone. It seems to have been a meaningful romance for both: her literary tastes influenced his own – thanks to Rowe, he became a serious reader – and in turn, Harry chronicled their year together, and subsequent breakup, on *Fine Line*. In 2019, *Rolling Stone* reported that, as per Tom Hull, their split had "a big impact" on Styles.

He and Olivia Wilde met in late 2020, when she directed him in the film *Don't Worry Darling* – he played the "mysterious" husband of Florence Pugh. They began dating early in 2021, and were together for two years, during which he got to know her two children. The reason for their split was the time-tested one of busy schedules keeping them apart.

A few months later, in March 2023, Styles was seen with model Emily Ratajkowski – a brief liaison that had special meaning for him: in the One Direction days, he'd called her his "celebrity crush". From late spring of that year, he and actress Taylor Russell were together and, if you believed social media, he was "smitten" until they broke up in May 2024.

Zoë Kravitz, actress daughter of rock star Lenny, came into Styles' life in the summer of 2025. They were soon, according to *Heat*, serious about each other, and the magazine claimed he was preparing to pop the question: "He wants to build something lasting and Zoë feels like the person to do it with." And Harry looks to be doing just that: news of the pair's engagement broke in April 2026.

Opposite: In New York with Zoë Kravitz on March 9, 2026, about a month before the couple's engagement was revealed.

KISS
PRADA

LG
ONE WAY

FINE LINE

Two and a half years elapsed between Styles's debut and his second album – a period spent touring the first LP and making *Fine Line* during gaps between his 89 tour dates. There was less at stake this time: *Harry Styles* had been a global hit, and he was now less worried about how to make a record with his name on it. In the event, writer/producer Tyler Johnson told him that he had to make the record *he* wanted to make – and that set him free to enjoy the process. Though it "only" reached No. 2 in the UK, *Fine Line* topped the charts nearly everywhere else.

SINGLE

RELEASED: DECEMBER 13, 2019
WRITERS: HARRY STYLES, THOMAS HULL, MITCH ROWLAND, TYLER JOHNSON
PRODUCER: TYLER JOHNSON
ALTERNATE VERSION: LIVE AT IHEARTRADIO JINGLE BALL

GOLDEN

The album opens with this euphoric, '70s-referencing pop morsel, which was released as the fifth of *Fine Line*'s seven singles. Its performance was fair to middling: 26 in the UK, 57 in the US.

Because it appeared 10 months after the album came out, towards the end of a long run of singles, it didn't get the attention it would have earlier in this era.

He knew all along that it would be the first track on the album because it was the first song he wrote, on the second day of the sessions. He and his collaborators were huddled around the kitchen table at Rick Rubin's Shangri-La Studios in Malibu, California, as Harry played it on guitar, and all of them were singing the harmonies. "The acoustics in the kitchen made it sound so cool, so we thought, 'This song's gonna work'," he told *Rolling Stone* in its December 13, 2019, issue.

As the song progressed, he and the band found themselves dancing around the studio, collectively ecstatic over what they were creating. "We'd dance around the studio and be, like, 'I love this! I don't know if it's good, I don't know if it's bad, but we love it'," he said during an onstage Q&A with *On Air with Ryan Seacrest* just before a secret iHeartRadio performance on February 29, 2020.

When he played his new music for people who hadn't yet heard it – people like, say, Rob Stringer, CEO of Sony Music Group, who'd instructed Styles to go and make a record, and not come back until he had something to play for him – this was the song he played. "We didn't set a deadline – if it wasn't going to be right in the way Harry wanted it, it wasn't going to come out," Stringer told *Music Week* several days before *Fine Line* appeared.

While the song *feels* incredibly buoyant, which led reviewers to praise its shimmering style – on December 13, *Popsugar* wrote: "The sunny pop song has a bit of an old-school vibe, and can we talk about the lovely backing vocals?" – its core meaning comes from a different emotional place. The lyric has Harry admitting to hopelessness and feeling broken, and during a November 22 interview with Apple Music's Zane Lowe, he was asked about that. "You said [earlier in the interview] that vulnerability is the way to great friendship," Lowe said. "I feel like ['Golden'] establishes that." Styles didn't disagree, but he did say that "Golden" was also a driving song. "I used to drive from here to the studio and listen to it and it's kind of like as soon as we had it, 'Golden' was the perfect PCH [Pacific Coast Highway] song. It feels so Malibu to me."

Opposite: Inducting his idol, Stevie Nicks, into the Rock & Roll Hall of Fame. Barclays Center, Brooklyn, March 29, 2019.

WATERMELON SUGAR

SINGLE

RELEASED: MAY 18, 2020 (SINGLE) / DECEMBER 13, 2019 (ALBUM)
WRITERS: HARRY STYLES, THOMAS HULL, TYLER JOHNSON, MITCH ROWLAND
PRODUCERS: TYLER JOHNSON, KID HARPOON

Styles has form when it comes to fruit songs, "Kiwi" being another, while strawberries have their moment in "Adore You". But only "Watermelon Sugar", an across-the-board Top 5 hit (and *Billboard* Hot 100 No. 1) has a lyric that *CNN Entertainment* decorously called "NSFW" when it broke this story on October 4, 2021.

It referred to a Styles show at the Bridgestone Arena in Nashville three days before, during his 169-date *Love on Tour* outing. It was during the encore; he'd finished "Sign of the Times" and was revving up for the next tune. "This is about... uh... the *sweetness* of life!" he announced, to appreciative cheers from the crowd. "It's also about the female orgasm, but that's totally different," he said, to much louder cheers. "It's not really relevant." (For what it's worth, he ended the encore fruitily, following "Watermelon Sugar" with "Kiwi".)

He'd been coyer when asked about it during November's Zane Lowe interview. Styles had performed the song on *Saturday Night Live* on November 16, "and everyone's kind of figured out what it's about," Lowe informed him. "Is that what it's about? I don't know," Styles countered.

Well, he'd admitted to *Rolling Stone* on August 26 that *Fine Line* as a whole was about "having sex and feeling sad". He'd also said its songs related to "personal heartbreak", from which many inferred he was talking about the end of his relationship with Camille Rowe, a French model with whom he split in 2018. Interviewed by *Elle* for its August 2017 issue, she'd answered a question about her favourite books, among which was *In Watermelon Sugar* by Richard Brautigan. Styles, an enthusiastic reader, must have borrowed the book when she'd finished it, because he brought it to a studio session in Nashville in September 2017. He was in the city to play the third show on his *Live on Tour* jaunt, and while there decided to check into The Cave – a studio belonging to Tyler Johnson – to see what he could come up with.

This was the result: a poppy track, made irresistibly danceable by the funky bassline that runs through it. Co-writer and co-producer Tom Hull related the story to *Music Week* in May 2021: "It was one of the first songs, it might even have been the first song, we wrote for the album. I was playing a riff, Tyler was doing some chords and then Harry turned up and started singing and the whole thing developed. He was reading a book called *In Watermelon Sugar*."

Amazingly, it was only intended to be a promo single, but then got a full release, sold 1 million copies and won a Grammy (Best Pop Solo Performance) and a Brit (Best British Single) in 2021.

Opposite above: At the 2019 Met Gala with then creative director of Gucci, Alessandro Michele.

Opposite below: Solo at the Met. New York, May 6, 2019.

1957

ADORE YOU

SINGLE

RELEASED: DECEMBER 6, 2019 (SINGLE) / DECEMBER 13, 2019 (ALBUM)
WRITERS: HARRY STYLES, THOMAS HULL, TYLER JOHNSON, AMY ALLEN
PRODUCER: KID HARPOON
ALTERNATE VERSION: OFFICIAL VIDEO EXTENDED VERSION

***Fine Line*'s second single went Top 10 on both sides of the Atlantic, and eventually sold 5 million certified units in the US and 1.8 million in Britain.**

As undeniably pleasant as it is to shift millions of downloads, Styles may have been almost as happy to learn that *The New York Times Magazine* included "Adore You" in a March 11, 2020, feature called "25 Songs That Matter Now". It was the third song in the list, just behind King Princess' "Prophet" and Tyler, The Creator's "Earfquake".

He was identified as "the [ex-One Directioner] people over 30 would recognize on the street", and the song was called "the album's defining single". (At the time the story was written, he'd put out three singles – "Golden", this one and "Falling". The song now regarded as the definitive single, "Watermelon Sugar", hadn't yet been released.)

"It's the [*Fine Line* track] in which past and present coalesce most seamlessly, its playful psychedelia streamlined into sleek modern hit-making. It lets Styles show off the full, androgynous range of his voice," the story went on. Perceptively, the *Times* recognized that Styles had become the sort of pop star that had few precedents: the androgyny, his interest in "what you'd almost have to call baby-boomer music" and his early-'70s-Mick-Jaggeresque dress sense.

As usual, Harry himself was elusive when asked about "Adore You". The lyric makes it pretty plain that it's a straightforward love song, written for someone he was exceptionally excited about.

Playing a *Tiny Desk* mini-show for American radio network NPR on March 16, however, he said, "It's about a fish" (the fish did have a co-starring role in the track's trippy video, and adding to the oddness, it contained a monologue by Rosalía). "I just had this fish and I really liked it and that's kind of the whole story." Relenting, he added that it was actually inspired by "that initial excitement of meeting someone... You're just, like, 'Take me!'"

"Adore You" was conceived during the last week of recording, in spring 2019. "He went through this breakup that had a big impact on him," Tom Hull told *Rolling Stone* in August 2019. "He had a whole emotional journey about her, this whole relationship. But I kept saying, 'The best way of dealing with it is to put it in these songs you're writing'." As with many musicians, Styles finds it easier to express his feelings in song lyrics rather than during interviews – he's certainly never told the media much about the relationship that spawned "Adore You".

Sticking with that resolution, he used another *Fine Line* track, "Falling" (see page 134), to "explain" the breakup with Camille Rowe – if, indeed, she was the woman who sent him on *Fine Line*'s "emotional journey".

Opposite: Clearly enjoying the Brit Awards with Jack Whitehall and Lizzo. O2 Arena, London, February 18, 2020.

LIGHTS UP

SINGLE

RELEASED: OCTOBER 11, 2019 (SINGLE) / DECEMBER 13, 2019 (ALBUM)
WRITERS: HARRY STYLES, THOMAS HULL, TYLER JOHNSON
PRODUCER: TYLER JOHNSON

Styles hadn't put out a single in two years – October 2017's "Kiwi" had been the last – when "Lights Up" dropped. It was the first taste of *Fine Line*, a record wildly anticipated: its name was first revealed by Styles via Twitter on November 4 – "FINE LINE. THE ALBUM. DEC 13" – and then the tracklisting on November 19.

Even without having heard any of the songs except "Lights Up", multiple media outlets ran stories with this same headline: "Here's Everything We Know About Harry Styles' New Album". What they knew was pretty limited: the title, song names and the cover art – a fisheye-lens photo of Styles recreating the 1970s in a pink satin blouse and high-waisted, wide-leg trousers. Some of the song titles, such as "To Be So Lonely" and "Treat People with Kindness", hinted at emotional times, but these were generally pretty bare-bones details. Styles, though, was now too important an artist to ignore bare-bones details. Proof of importance: a few days before *Fine Line*'s release, this single, which had been out for two months, had 138,842,763 Spotify streams to its name.

There was also in "Lights Up" an intriguing first single. The release timing, first of all: October 11, 2019, was National Coming Out Day, and naming the song "Lights Up" seemed a directive to raise your cigarette lighter, torch, matches. The music itself was jubilant and attention-seeking, and its psychedelic/soulful mood overwhelmingly positive.

"'Lights Up' is deliciously unsubtle", *Vulture* declared in an October 11 review, which touched on the lyrics, and their demand that listeners find their own light and shine in its glow – and it also remarked on the video, part of which is set at "a steamy party with bodies gently jostling and caressing each other, where our protagonist snuggles with men and women". Another review on the same day, in *Paper*, said more or less the same thing: "Harry Styles is drenched, tripping and maybe coming out in his new video." (Drenched: he was soaked in sweat. Tripping: he'd told interviewers that he'd tried magic mushrooms for the first time while making the album, and had enjoyed the experience. Coming out: he's never said in so many words.)

"Lights Up" was written in the last week of studio sessions, in the spring of 2019. He and the band had one late surge of creativity, and there the songs were. Styles knew that in "Lights Up" he'd made the necessary swaying arm-waver – an anthem, basically – to reintroduce himself. When he played it to his label, he was succinct. In a December 13 interview with *Rolling Stone* he described the scene: "I told them, 'This is the first single. It's two minutes thirty-five. You're welcome.'"

Opposite: Not his bedroom, not his diving helmet. Pre-release listening party for *Fine Line* in Los Angeles, December 11, 2019.

Spotify

ALBUM TRACK

CHERRY

RELEASED: DECEMBER 13, 2019
WRITERS: HARRY STYLES, THOMAS HULL, TYLER JOHNSON, JEFF BHASKER, SAMMY WITTE
PRODUCERS: TYLER JOHNSON, SAMMY WITTE
ALTERNATE VERSION: *VOGUE* ACOUSTIC PERFORMANCE

There are two potential outcomes when, refreshed after a few pints, people sit down in the middle of the night to compose a song. They either wake up the next morning, listen to the fruits of their labours and decide they really shouldn't drunk-write – or they wake up and decide the hangover is worth it. "Cherry" is an example of the latter.

Tom Hull told *Music Week* on February 18, 2020, that it had been "written at one in the morning, with Sammy [Witte, co-writer/co-producer], Tyler and Harry, a bottle of tequila down"; more specifically, Witte was playing acoustic guitar, and strummed a riff that Harry thought was similar to one played by John Lennon on the *White Album*. He loves The Beatles. Then next thing they knew, they'd made a song called "Cherry". (Yes, another metaphor expressed through fruit.)

"The night that I wrote it, I was saying that I was feeling a lot of pressure," Styles revealed to Zane Lowe on November 22. "I was, like, 'I feel like this record has to be really big. So I feel like I need to make certain songs.' And Tyler said to me, 'You just have to make the record that you want to make right now.' So we stayed up and wrote 'Cherry' that night."

The track is airy, dreamy – part folk, thanks to a gently picked guitar, and part electronica, thanks to Harry's woozy, filtered voice. It immediately makes an impression: in a March 2026 retrospective feature, *Rolling Stone* called it *Fine Line*'s "most powerful moment", while *Esquire* pronounced it "the set standout" in December 2019.

But this isn't just another Harry heartbreak song. Though it brims with the sadness, crossed wires and regret that characterize several other songs on *Fine Line* (see "Falling" and "To Be So Lonely"), "Cherry" is much more intimate and personal than any other album track. For the first time, Styles dispenses with his habitual opaqueness about relationships, and directly refers to the woman who broke his heart. Not only does he refer to her, she's on the song.

Camille Rowe – for she does seem to be the mystery woman – is the female voice saying "Coucou" ("Hello") at the start, and closing the track with a recording of herself speaking on the phone in French. It's been claimed it was a voicemail for Styles, but he was in the room with her when it happened. "I was playing guitar and she took a phone call, and she was actually speaking in the key of the song," he told *Rolling Stone*. The pair were on friendly terms by the time "Cherry" was written, and Camille gave him permission to use the recording.

Opposite: Performing at the Brit Awards. 02 Arena, London, February 18, 2020

SINGLE

RELEASED: MARCH 7, 2020 (SINGLE) / DECEMBER 13, 2019 (ALBUM)
WRITERS: HARRY STYLES, THOMAS HULL
PRODUCER: KID HARPOON

FALLING

Fine Line's third single, "Falling" captures the self-loathing that follows a breakup caused by one party's thoughtlessness. Styles is the party, and this piano ballad, written with Tom Hull, is his unsparing audit of his behaviour.

It begins with him lying in bed, brooding about the absence of his ex-girlfriend, who has only recently become his ex. She's left him, and "Falling" is devoted to explaining why. (He got drunk and cheated.) He doesn't spare his own feelings – if the ex hates him, he hates himself more.

He and Hull were the only writers on the track (which was produced by Hull under his Kid Harpoon nom de pop), making it the album's only song not credited to three or more writers. (Hull co-authored 11 of its 12 songs, signalling a close friendship with Styles. Interviewed by *Music Week* on February 18, 2020, Hull characterized it as a best friends relationship, valued by Styles because, for one thing, Hull was older – by 12 years – and "at a different point in my life… I've got two kids at home and I'm more settled, so I have time to think differently." Styles and Hull are still tight enough for Hull to have co-written and/or co-produced every song on the roaringly successful album, *Kiss All the Time. Disco, Occasionally.*)

It was written during the spring of 2019, at Harry's Los Angeles house. He'd asked Hull for a lift, and was in the shower when he arrived. Hull seated himself at Styles' piano and when he emerged from the shower, Hull began to noodle around on the keyboard. "… and we wrote it there," Styles told *Rolling Stone* in December 2019. "So I was completely naked when I wrote that song." (One wonders whether provocative comments like this speak to Styles' sense of mischief, or just a determination not to be boring.)

Hull told *Music Week*: "I popped up there and he was getting out of the shower. I started playing piano while I was waiting for him, he was singing and in an hour we had written 'Falling'." Styles remembered it as 20 minutes; either way, it was a very quick birth.

The lyric cycles from loneliness – a longtime Styles song topic – to an admission of guilt to an apology for saying something stupid to an existential "Who am I?" – and back again. It sounds as if, unhappy as he is about losing his girlfriend, he's more disturbed by the person he might become. He told Zane Lowe in November 2019 that while making *Fine Line* he was either euphorically happy or "the lowest I've ever felt in my life". He feared "falling back into one of those [moods]."

Opposite: Styles performs on the *Today* show on a chilly New York morning. Rockefeller Plaza, Manhattan, February 26, 2020.

Overleaf: Total confidence: playing for SiriusXM and Pandora Secret Session at the Music Hall of Williamsburg, Brooklyn, February 28, 2020.

itibank

SEQUENTIAL

TO BE SO LONELY

ALBUM TRACK

RELEASED: DECEMBER 13, 2019
WRITERS: HARRY STYLES, THOMAS HULL, TYLER JOHNSON, MITCH ROWLAND
PRODUCERS: TYLER JOHNSON, KID HARPOON

This is a sort of answer song to "Falling", or perhaps it's the second half of it. The first line even contains the word "falling". (He says it's not his fault he fell for the woman in question.) On the earlier song, he confessed to having played around while under the influence; here, he's been drunk-dialling.

Going by his own lyrics, alcohol played a part in some poor decisions – he's certainly not alone there – but on this track he's defiant about it. The entire first verse finds him shifting the blame for having fallen in love in the first place. It's not his fault. It's somebody else's. The same goes for the tipsy post-relationship phone calls. Nowt to do with him.

Of course, he knows that's not true. The entirety of "To be So Lonely" plays out like a therapy session: he admits he's done wrong, tries to justify it, then claims he's a big-headed so-and-so who refuses ever to apologize. He's jealous by nature (and it's not easy being perpetually jealous, he sighs). He acknowledges that his ex is trying to do the right thing – she's offering friendship, but he can't accept it yet. The song ends with him sinking into a morass of loneliness – yet there's a hint in there that, having gone through a self-reflection process in this song, he might be nearing a turning point.

Despite the emotional turmoil of the lyric, Styles considered "To be So Lonely" "one of my favourites to work on [on the album]," he said just before playing it at his March 2020 *Tiny Desk* session. And from a musical point of view, his enthusiasm is understandable – the scene is set at the start with flamenco-style strumming and a gliding bass melody, but the minimalism only lasts until the pre-chorus. There it expands into a much bigger thing, with harmonies and a wide-open, Spanish-jam-session ambience – and the flamenco strumming carries the song along throughout, endowing it with the nostalgia of a lovely sunset.

This was "one of the first all-nighter, through-the-night songs" he made while recording at Peter Gabriel's studio, Real World, in Bath. (In a doff of the cap to Gabriel, he covered his 1986 hit single "Sledgehammer" when he guested on Howard Stern's radio show on March 2, 2020.)

Styles credits guitarist Mitch Rowland with the song's genesis. "He sent me a voicenote, and it was essentially the whole song," he revealed on *Tiny Desk*. That included the flamenco effect, which Rowland played on a six-string ukulele called a guitalele. Having heard the music, Harry tucked himself into a corner "and sat there with headphones and did the melody and the lyrics and it was pretty fast."

Opposite: At the 2021 Grammy Awards, where he won Best Pop Solo Performance for "Watermelon Sugar". Los Angeles, March 14, 2021.

ALBUM TRACK

RELEASED: DECEMBER 13, 2019
WRITERS: HARRY STYLES, THOMAS HULL, MITCH ROWLAND, JEFF BHASKER
PRODUCER: KID HARPOON

SHE

"She" is nothing less than "a deranged six-minute space-sex trip that feels like Prince jamming with Pink Floyd," *Rolling Stone* memorably wrote in March 2026. That hits the nail on the head – it's trippy, woozy and laced with a Mitch Rowland guitar journey to inner space.

And at 6.02 minutes, it's the second-longest number on the album. "[Mitch] was a little, uh, influenced," Styles said in a December 2019 *Rolling Stone* interview. "He was on mushrooms. We all were. We had no idea what we were doing."

The six weeks he and the band spent at Shangri-La in 2019 influenced Styles' state of mind, as did the fact that they never once went to Los Angeles. Although the city was just 28 miles away, to have gone there, even for an afternoon, would have marred what Styles had come to think of as his Golden State idyll. Friends visited with their kids and dogs, and the whole crew played games and swam in the Pacific. The experience, including the mushrooms, made him reconsider who he was – he'd already started to practise transcendental meditation, and the Shangri-La lifestyle meshed with his new state of consciousness.

Thus, "She" was the product of a freshly "enlightened" Styles. He doesn't say whether he'd used mushrooms before, but at the Shangri-La sessions they were an aid to both relaxation and creativity. He and the others would lie in the grass out back, within sight of the ocean, have their mushrooms and listen to Paul McCartney's *Ram* album. Once, he told *Rolling Stone* in August 2019, he bit off the tip of his tongue. (Remarkably, Mick Jagger, who's seen by many as an influence on Harry's androgynous style, did the same in a sports accident when he was 16.) "So I was trying to sing with all this blood gushing out of my mouth. So many fond memories, this place."

After recording "She" he forgot about it, and when he returned to it some time later, he was both bemused and bowled over. The song was "phenomenal", he thought, but Rowland couldn't remember what he'd played, so he had to learn it from the tape. They got there in the end.

"She" evokes golden afternoons and fantasies of escape from the nine-to-five – and it's relatively safe to say that escape is exactly what it's about. The lyric, which Styles has never explained, seems to depict a typical nine-to-fiver – kids, a desk job, a PA who brings him coffee – who daydreams about a woman he calls She, and of fleeing his restrictive life.

When Styles was weighing up the songs they'd done, deciding which would make it onto the album, "She" was always among the first on his list.

Opposite: Enjoying an iHeartRadio Secret Session at the Bowery Ballroom. New York, February 29, 2020.

novation

SUNFLOWER, VOL. 6

ALBUM TRACK

RELEASED: DECEMBER 13, 2019
WRITERS: HARRY STYLES, THOMAS HULL, GREG KURSTIN
PRODUCER: GREG KURSTIN
ALTERNATE VERSION: SOUNDCLOUD A CAPPELLA VERSION

It's no coincidence that "Sunflower, Vol. 6" follows "She". Together, they comprise the album's weirdest/artiest/most psychedelic (delete to taste) 10 minutes, and they fit together like a frozen margarita (the band's cocktail of choice while working at Shangri-La) and an achingly beautiful Malibu sunset.

Considering how seamlessly they work, it's something of a surprise that, rather than being produced by "She"'s Kid Harpoon, "Sunflower" was overseen by Greg Kurstin – a nine-time Grammy winner and the guy tapped up when superleague talents (Adele, et al) have an album that needs producing.

This one was produced at Kurstin's own studio in Los Angeles, rather than at Shangri-La, and Kurstin added his own touch to the track. Like "She", it stirs thoughts of the Summer of Love – the fabled time in 1967 when the West Coast was a magnet for "alternative" types, and days were long and golden. But it has its own identity, too: Kurstin brought his own toolkit of effects to the song, and uses them from the first moment. Literally: the song begins with backmasking – reversing the tape, a traditional way to signal "weird times ahead". The distorted sound it creates is Styles saying "sunflower". Then Kurstin turns in "an absolutely batsh*t performance on clavichord that gives the song a blend of playfulness and unbeatable musicality", as *Vulture* put it in a December 2019 album review.

There are elements of reggae and township jive in there, too, and Harry's vocal is put through an interesting wringer at times. There's a phaser effect, and in the final 30 seconds he produces a succession of operatic whoops. It's really some tune.

The lyric at the heart of this is much smaller and more personal than all the activity surrounding it. "Sunflower" is his name for the woman who inspired the song – to Styles, she has the light-reflecting beauty and openness of a sunflower. The relationship seems to be ongoing; he writes about their mutual love, and little shared moments, like dancing in the kitchen. He sings about their hearing dancehall together, a clear reference to the song's touch of reggae.

By this time, Styles had a new No. 1 fan: Stevie Nicks. They'd been friends since 2015, when he presented her with a carrot cake – he'd personally piped her name in icing on top – after a Fleetwood Mac show in London. "'Sunflower'" is such a great little song," she told *Vogue* in November 2020. She had her own idea of how the music video should look: "You're gonna be a bee, and the sunflower would be your girlfriend, and you guys would get married and live in a beehive," she told him. It's a small tragedy that it was never made.

Opposite: Beware flying boas! At the Grammy Awards, Los Angeles Convention Center, on March 14, 2021.

CANYON MOON

ALBUM TRACK

RELEASED: DECEMBER 13, 2019
WRITERS: HARRY STYLES, THOMAS HULL, MITCH ROWLAND
PRODUCER: KID HARPOON

Harry is one of those Brits who, when introduced to the Southern California lifestyle, takes to it straightaway. Even before launching his solo career, he owned a house in the Hollywood Hills – a four-bed, six-bath pad he paid $6.8 million for in 2016. (He sold it for $6 million in 2019 when he found he was using it less than he'd expected to.) "Canyon Moon" is the result of his love affair with the place.

Even the title is redolent of SoCal: canyons are a prominent geological feature of the LA area, and Styles has ties to two. There's Beachwood Canyon, which pops up in "Falling" – it mentions the Beachwood Café, a local hangout that came to worldwide attention after being included in the lyric – and Laurel Canyon, home of his idol Joni Mitchell. Either canyon could be the one in the title, but the betting is on Laurel. It has the edge because in December 2019 Styles described the track to *Rolling Stone* as "Crosby, Stills & Nash on steroids" – and Mitchell's then-boyfriend, Graham Nash, lived here with her in the late '60s.

"Canyon Moon" is both sweet and bittersweet: it's folky, strummy, mellow and infused with longing. Styles is in Europe, visiting Paris and Rome, and all the while he's nostalgic, remembering the beauty of watching the moon on a Laurel Canyon evening with a former partner. She introduced him to the '60s music she loved (which he himself grew to love), and even if they're no longer together, he remembers their time lovingly. He thinks of the canyon as home, and in the refrain tells himself, over and over, that he's going back as soon as he can.

"I was in a pretty big Joni hole," he told *Rolling Stone*. Such a big one that he and Tom Hull sought out Joellen Lapidus, the dulcimer-maker who introduced the stringed instrument to Mitchell. It features on one of Styles' favourite Mitchell albums, *Blue*, and he was enchanted by it. Lapidus made him an Appalachian dulcimer, the variety Mitchell used, and gave him an introductory lesson. Its guitar-like sound is all over "Canyon Moon".

Above: At the Los Angeles premiere of *My Policeman*, November 1, 2022.

Opposite: A year earlier, on the set of the film, in which Styles played a closeted officer.

In the second verse, Styles muses about a Canyon friend named Jenny. It wasn't until March 2026, just before the release of *Kiss All the Time. Disco, Occasionally.*, that he explained "Jenny" to Apple Music's Zane Lowe. She was Tom Hull's wife, Jenny Myles – and after he namechecked her, their son, Fox, was jealous, and demanded the same treatment. "He was playing football, and [said], 'If I hit the crossbar, will you put my name in a song?' I [said], 'I'll give you three tries'." Which is why "Dance No More", from *KATTDO*, contains the word Fox.

POLICE · PUBLIC

TREAT PEOPLE WITH KINDNESS

SINGLE

RELEASED: JANUARY 9, 2021 (SINGLE) / DECEMBER 13, 2019 (ALBUM)
WRITERS: HARRY STYLES, JEFF BHASKER, ILSEY JUBER
PRODUCER: JEFF BHASKER

"Treat people with kindness" is a worthy directive, but it's often treated as a catchphrase by people who say it but don't do it. Styles isn't one of them. For him, the phrase is nothing less than a mantra.

What started out as a badge worn on his guitar strap – the original said "TPWK" and was followed by another that spelled out the message – became a quest for him. He wanted to grab the catchphrase and make it meaningful.

The fandom have been happy to help it along, wearing pins and T-shirts that he made available at merch stands on his first arena tour in 2018. "Harries", as his fans are known, are renowned as one of pop's most inclusive fandoms, and for their commitment to the same principles followed by Styles: he urges all to be their authentic selves, and allow others to be who they are.

The logical follow-through? He wrote a song about it. It remained an unrealized intention for quite a while, though, until he ran the idea past Jeff Bhasker. Should he write a tune called "Treat People with Kindness"? Bhasker was warmly encouraging. Of course he should, and Bhasker would help to write it. Styles still hesitated because it touched something unfamiliar in his psyche, "but then I wanted to lean into that. I feel like that song opened something that's been in my core," he told *Rolling Stone* in December 2019.

The number he wrote with Bhasker and Ilsey Juber (songwriter daughter of former Wings guitarist Laurence Juber, who played on the track) is unlike anything else on *Fine Line*. On an album full of unexpected twists and turns, "Treat People with Kindness" might be the twistiest. Who, after all, expected him to come up with a Broadway showtune? It's brassy and upbeat, and sent soaring skyward by a gospel choir – all that's missing is an actual Broadway show.

The video, made early in 2020, does its best to be that show. It was based on a 1920s clip of the celebrated American dance duo the Nicholas Brothers that co-director Gabe Turner happened to see – he instantly envisaged a Styles video based on the same idea. Harry is partnered in it by Phoebe Waller-Bridge, whom he met when he saw her one-woman *Fleabag* live show in the summer of 2019. He plays a glitter-suited nightclub hoofer who charms club patron Waller-Bridge into joining him onstage, where they do fancy footwork in front of a chorus line. They twirl and leap as the backing vocalists urge us to look for the good in everything. Filmed in black-and-white at Troxy in East London, it's a brilliant showpiece. It was moderately successful as a single, but great fun as a song.

Opposite: Winning the British Single award for "Watermelon Sugar" at the 2021 Brit Awards. 02 Arena, London, May 11, 2021.

FINE LINE

SINGLE

RELEASED: NOVEMBER 19, 2021 (SINGLE) / DECEMBER 13, 2019 (ALBUM)
WRITERS: HARRY STYLES, THOMAS HULL, MITCH ROWLAND, TYLER JOHNSON, SAMMY WITTE
PRODUCERS: KID HARPOON, TYLER JOHNSON

Almost from the time he wrote it, in January 2018, Styles knew this would be *Fine Line*'s closing track (it was also the seventh and last single from the album).

Though he'd barely started work on the album ("Fine Line" was either the first or second song he wrote for it – he's said it was the first, but on a different occasion also claimed the same of "Golden"), he already had a feeling about the track.

Answering fans' questions on Capital FM in March 2020, he explained that even in its embryonic state, "it felt like it described… the process of making it and how the album felt in terms of different kind of songs on it."

In terms of "describing the process of making" the album, he already knew that the second album would be different from the debut – because, as he's said, he wasn't squeezed by the pressure he felt while making the first. "Fine Line" can be taken as a symbol of his maturing into a confident solo artist, unafraid to try dozens of ideas.

Track co-writer Tom Hull said as much to *Music Week* in April 2020. "Harry is very creative. What I love about him is that he is full of ideas." Styles wasn't one of those artists who treats it as a job, turning up at a studio at 10am and reluctantly switching into songwriting mode. (Hull discreetly didn't name names.) "It's non-stop working when we're in the studio. It's constant." Even between album cycles, he sends piano and lyric ideas to Hull, who says Styles simply doesn't stop working.

It was at Hull's house in Los Angeles that "Fine Line" began, during a gap in the 2017/18 *Live on Tour* excursion. Styles initially envisaged it as a simple folk song, but it grew and grew; his vocals were layered, horn effects were added and cymbal crashes were used as punctuation. Later, while working on the track at Peter Gabriel's studio in Bath, they added a piano coda played by writer/engineer Sammy Witte – it fit Styles' idea of "a big, epic outro," he told *Rolling Stone* in December 2019.

When he began writing the track, his relationship with Camille Rowe was ongoing; the pair had reached the inevitable stage of realizing, despite hopes to the contrary, that neither of them was perfect. "Fine Line" acknowledges the love Styles still lavishes on Rowe, but also the bickering and their failure to adequately communicate. Sometimes he hates her, he sings, but he also adores her. They're treading a fine line, but Styles wants to believe they'll come through it intact. That's how the song, and his second album, end: with Styles telling himself that all will be fine.

Opposite: Performing at his Harryween fancy-dress shows at Madison Square Garden, New York on October 31, 2021 (**above**). and October 30, 2021 (**below**).

Overleaf: Kicking off the 169-date *Love on Tour* run at the MGM Grand Garden Arena, Las Vegas, on September 4, 2021.

STYLES ON TOUR

"I finished my last tour in 2023, and after that I took a bunch of time off. I realized I'd spent half my life in music – touring, creating albums and making songs about fruit that people think are about sex," Styles said during his opening monologue as guest host of *Saturday Night Live* on March 14, 2026. Albums and fruit are the less-demanding parts of what he's been doing since he was 16 – it's touring that's really made itself felt. It wasn't the actual shows so much as the travelling that weighed on him, affecting everything from his mental health to his social life. After the 2021–23 *Love on Tour* run, he revealed that because the schedule had been so punishing, he'd declined invitations from friends during weeks off, just to be sure he rested.

He hosted *SNL* towards the end of the gap between *Love on Tour*, which finished on July 22, 2023, in Reggio Emilia, and the start of 2026's *Together, Together* trek, which began in Amsterdam on May 16. The framework of *Together, Together* (named after "Forever Forever", an instrumental he performed on the piano in Reggio) was the perfect bounce-back answer to *Love on Tour*. First, there were only 67 shows – a third of *Love on Tour*'s 169. (There were 89 on his debut solo jaunt, 2017–18's *Live on Tour*.) But the real advantage was that instead of visiting 67 different cities, *Together, Together* was a seven-site enterprise. Just seven cities hosted the tour, and each had Styles for a residency of between two and 30 dates.

The idea was to settle down in one place for an extended period and let the people come to him. In a March 4 review of *Kiss All the Time.*, *The Guardian* wrote, "North America is covered by a staggering 30 dates at New York's Madison Square Garden. The expectation seemed to be that Styles' fans are so devoted, they'll cross the country to see him, rather than vice versa." The expectation was well-founded: there were 11.5 million pre-sale registrations for around 550,000 tickets.

Starting with One Direction, Styles quickly got used to life on the road. He had to: 1D toured every year of their existence, rolling through *Up All Night* (2011–12), *Take Me Home* (2013), *Where We Are* (2014) and 2015's *On the Road Again*. (is it possible that the name of the last was a touch sardonic, given that they'd hardly been *off* the road during the previous four years?)

Still, it was useful training for the day that Styles would be carrying shows on his own. It had helped a great deal that he learned performance skills as one of five: "When you're in a band with four other people, there's so much room to hide [onstage]. There's only ever so much weight that's on your shoulders," Styles told *The Sunday Times Magazine* in February 2026. "The first couple of times on stage [alone], I'd think, 'What do I do with my hands?' [And] I also felt very alone all of a sudden."

Gruelling as touring can be, he's still happy to be able to do it; it's a necessary part of what he considers the best job in the world. At the end of the Reggio show, he made a tearful speech to the 100,000-strong audience. "Thank you for the way you've supported me over the last 13 years. I couldn't have done it without you and for loving me in the way that you have. Thank you so much. I am so full right now. I've never been happier in my life."

Opposite: Carrying off purple better than any artist since Prince. Radio 1's Big Weekend 2022 in Coventry, May 29, 2022.

HARRY'S HOUSE

Two and a half years elapsed between *Fine Line* and the Grammy-winning (Album of the Year, Pop Vocal Album) *Harry's House*, during which the Covid pandemic imposed "a big phase of self-reflection", as Styles said during an *Apple Music* interview on May 16, 2022. The album that came out of it was intimate, and very much formed by having spent time alone, processing his feelings about – among other things – his lack of privacy and the constant speculation about his life. Released on May 20, 2022, *Harry's House* was an across-the-board No. 1. It's since gone double platinum in the US and triple platinum in the UK.

MUSIC FOR A SUSHI RESTAURANT

SINGLE

RELEASED: OCTOBER 3, 2022 (SINGLE) / MAY 20, 2022 (ALBUM)
WRITERS: HARRY STYLES, TOM HULL, TYLER JOHNSON, MITCH ROWLAND
PRODUCERS: KID HARPOON, TYLER JOHNSON
ALTERNATE VERSION: *ONE NIGHT ONLY IN NEW YORK*

The album's first song (and third single), "Music for a Sushi Restaurant", has an arty ring to it – and that's just the title.

It's the sort of name you might find in the tracklisting of an album by synth pioneer Brian Eno, but here it is, the opening tune on the third solo album by an increasingly experimental Harry Styles.

The title was literally inspired by a dinner at a Los Angeles sushi place. Styles was there with "my producer" (either Kid Harpoon or Tyler Johnson, who co-produced the entire album), and was bemused when a song from *Fine Line* came on during their meal. "I said, 'This is really strange music for a sushi restaurant,'" he told NPR on the album's release day. "And then I [said], 'Oh, that'd be a really fun album title.'"

Cooler heads must have prevailed, because the album ended up being called *Harry's House*, but that's got a quirky origin story in its own right: the 1973 debut album by one of Japan's most influential musicians, Haruomi Hosono, was called *Hosono House*. Styles heard and loved it while in Japan, and thought *Harry's House* would make an excellent title for his own album. Slightly awkwardly, Joni Mitchell appeared to think he'd named the record after the song "Harry's House/Centerpiece" from her 1975 album *The Hissing of Summer Lawns*; when Styles tweeted his album's name, Mitchell tweeted back, "love the title", and typed out her song's first four lines.

The music itself is as left-field as the title. It's a finger-popping synth-jazz piece that has Styles scatting – singing wordless syllables – for the first time. "You know, you have a line of lyric that you don't know, and you go [scats a line from the song's second verse] instead, and it was, like, 'This is fun as hell'," he recounted to *Apple Music*. The rest of the lyric – the non-scatted sections – is one bounteous food metaphor. Ice cream, eggs, bubblegum and fried rice are all deployed as Styles tries to impress a love interest with his desire for her.

Written during the early stages of making the album, the song was eventually picked as the opening track thanks to the reactions of friends when Styles played it to them. He knew he had a hit when all asked to hear more of the song – "It's, like, how do you want to set the tone?" he told Apple Music.

The brilliant video, directed by Aube Perrie, takes Styles' interest in surrealism to a higher plane altogether. Harry stars as a merman – half Styles, half squid – who washes ashore and is taken to a kitchen where chefs prepare to turn him into sushi. Deservedly, the single hit No. 3 in the UK and No. 8 in the US.

Opposite: Could life be any better for a boy from Holmes Chapel? Onstage at Coachella. California, April 15, 2022.

LATE NIGHT TALKING

SINGLE

RELEASED: JUNE 21, 2022 (SINGLE) / MAY 20, 2022 (ALBUM)
WRITERS: HARRY STYLES, TOM HULL
PRODUCERS: KID HARPOON, TYLER JOHNSON
ALTERNATE VERSIONS: CASTLE OF DOOM LIVE, *ONE NIGHT ONLY IN NEW YORK*, RADIO 1 LIVE LOUNGE

This was the first song written for the album, apparently on the very day Harry and his collaborators moved into Shangri-La, the Malibu studio where they'd recorded a good bit of *Fine Line*.

The crew hadn't finished setting up the gear before Styles was sitting down with Tom Hull and sketching out this track. Even in its earliest form, the pair had an idea that it was pretty good, and that was hugely encouraging: it was as if they'd been holding their breath, and now they could exhale.

"It let us like relax a little bit – like, okay, if there's nothing else, we feel like we did some work," he reported on May 24, 2022, during a performance at Radio 1's Live Lounge. "The song's a lot of fun and I've enjoyed dancing to it many a time." It shaped their intentions for the rest of the record, he added, though he didn't clarify whether they had already had some idea of how they wanted *Harry's House* to sound, or whether "Late Night Talking" really did serve as the guidepost. He did tell *Better Homes & Gardens*' June 2022 issue that before starting the LP sessions, he'd deliberately avoided listening to any music but classical, so he could begin with "a blank canvas".

So the creation of "Late Night Talking" was a "moment of groove" during which he and Hull were creatively attuned, and it looks as if the song's album-directing breeziness was the right thing both for the song itself – sending it to No. 2 in the UK and No. 3 in the US – and for the LP as a whole. A review in *The Age* approvingly said: "This is an album of freewheeling effortlessness, of sensuality and confidence, of pop and R&B." The review went on to describe the song – a "glossy R&B shifter" – in slightly suggestive terms: "Shyness is not on the agenda. Reticence is out the door."

Relax; the track is completely SFW, though watching its video in a public place may be mildly embarrassing if others see the scenes of Styles sharing beds with gorgeous women who are intent on snuggling with each other as well as him (don't judge; it was in the name of art). At one point, he's in an actual art gallery, sprawled across what looks like Tracey Emin's installation, *My Bed*.

The theme of the song, and its ear-candy chorus, is the sweet nothings exchanged by lovers when in bed. Harry and his honey are in the infatuation stage, and he's realized he's in love. He debuted the song in April 2022, during his first appearance at Coachella, and because film director Olivia Wilde, his then-girlfriend, was there, fans decided it was about her. As for Harry, he's saying nothing.

Opposite above: Styles guests on SiriusXM's *The Howard Stern Show* in New York on May 18, 2022.

Opposite below: Pretty in pink: headlining the second weekend of Coachella. California, April 22, 2022.

Overleaf: One of many spectacular moments during his Coachella headline show. California, April 15, 2022.

SiriusXm
SiriusXm
SiriusXm
HOWARD
STERN
HOWARD
STERN
HOWARD
STERN

GRAPEJUICE

ALBUM TRACK

RELEASED: MAY 20, 2022
WRITERS: HARRY STYLES, TOM HULL, TYLER JOHNSON
PRODUCERS: KID HARPOON, TYLER JOHNSON
ALTERNATE VERSION: *ONE NIGHT ONLY IN NEW YORK*

When writing this, did Styles have what Diana Ross might call a love hangover? The question arises because the "grape juice" of the title is wine – red wine, specifically; according to the lyric, he doesn't drink white or rosé, and it seems to play a regular part in the narrator's life.

Whether he's dependent on it is hard to say – clues in the song hint that he might be. In the first verse, he's striding out on a beautiful afternoon, on the way to a florist's where he'll buy flowers for his lover. Then they'll go to "the heath" – possibly Hampstead Heath, near his London home – and have a romantic time. To this character, who's joyously in love, that feels like the perfect day.

But en route to the shop he changes his mind. Instead of flowers he buys a bottle of red. Here the song's meaning gets murky: is the "you" of the lyric his girlfriend or the wine? He reminisces about "you" accompanying him on his travels, and exults in time spent with "you". He likes a 1982 vintage, which shows he knows his grape juice; it was a well-balanced and superior year for Bordeaux, particularly. But the downside is that the hangovers are worse than they used to be, and he now needs the vino to make it through the day.

Interviewing Styles for Apple Music on May 16, 2022, Zane Lowe jestingly called "Grapejuice" "a beautiful tribute to dependency to alcohol and the hangover that follows" – but he was also quick to praise it for the "early McCartneyesque vibe" to Styles' voice, and the "really lovely four-on-the-floor midtempo groove". McCartney and his former band are a point of reference in other reviews, too: *Variety* noted the track's "Beatlesy" flavour, and *The Guardian* pinpointed "the McCartney-esque bass fills and Mellotron of 'Grapejuice'".

The song ambles along, borne by waves of the aforementioned Mellotron and Styles' hazy vocal, AutoTuned at times. It deftly captures the feel of a summer's day that's so beautiful it needs to be celebrated with a drink, but the consequent mellowness leads to brooding.

This song is relatively buried away, inasmuch as Styles rarely plays it live – he performed it on a couple of *Harry's House* promotional shows (see Alternate Version, above) but rarely since.

By the way, Styles doesn't bring grape juice on tour. Not only does he not drink on the road, he goes to bed early so he can get the 11 hours' sleep that keeps him going through show after show. He told Lowe, "For a couple of hours a night I give it everything and the rest of the time I'll spend trying to take care of myself."

Opposite: Rehearsing at Rockefeller Plaza for an appearance on *Today*, May 19, 2022 (**above**) and the televised broadcast (**below**).

AS IT WAS

SINGLE

RELEASED: APRIL 1, 2022 (SINGLE) / MAY 20, 2022 (ALBUM)
WRITERS: HARRY STYLES, TOM HULL, TYLER JOHNSON
PRODUCERS: KID HARPOON, TYLER JOHNSON
ALTERNATE VERSION: *ONE NIGHT ONLY IN NEW YORK*

Even non-fans know "As It Was". It would be almost impossible not to know the biggest-selling single of 2022 – the one that topped charts around the world and took Styles – already slightly successful – to a different level of stardom.

In Britain "As It Was" spent 10 weeks at No. 1, and its performance in the US was even more spectacular: 15 weeks at the top, making it the longest-lasting chart-topper ever by a British act, and the fourth-longest in history.

How did it manage this feat? Apart from the undeniable quality of the track, it was released strategically. It came out on April 1, 2022, his first new music since *Fine Line*'s album cycle had ended the previous autumn with the release of its title track. On April 15, he played it during his inaugural Coachella headline set. It was already No. 1 then, in both the US and the UK, but the prestige of performing at Coachella won it extra attention. Five weeks after that, on May 20, *Harry's House* was released and entered multiple international charts at No. 1. If Styles and "As It Was" weren't the hottest thing in pop at that point, they were when the genius of releasing it on April 1 became apparent. Pop loves nothing so much as a summer hit, and this synth-pop track had "huge summer banger" written all over it: ebullient, impossibly catchy and dreamily sung by Styles.

And that's before we reckon with the lyric, which, he told *Audacy Check In* in April, was about "metamorphosis and embracing change". He makes himself vulnerable, admitting that friends are worried about him, and seemingly expressing doubt about his then-relationship with Olivia Wilde. He described the track to Apple Music as "bittersweet... to me, it's really devastating. And it was very much written that way. I have the voicenote of it being written and it's very [downbeat]." So the character in the song is weighed down by worries, but they're offset by the delicious meringue of a melody. (Astonishingly, he later said he'd been unsure whether the track should be on the album.)

Styles wrote "As It Was" during the pandemic. He, Hull and Johnson had created a social bubble at Rob Stringer's house in Henley-on-Thames, in Oxfordshire – they were nearing the end of the album sessions and the Sony Music CEO had invited them to stay and use his place as a rehearsal room and studio. "Harry was sitting on the Moog One and I liked what he was playing, so I sat down and played as he started to write the melodies and the lyrics," Johnson told *Music Week* in October 2022.

They didn't know it, but they were composing the last song written for the album – and the biggest single of that year.

Opposite: Showing off impressive knuckledusters at Radio 1's Big Weekend at War Memorial Park. Coventry, May 29, 2022.

ALBUM TRACK

RELEASED: MAY 20, 2022
WRITERS: HARRY STYLES, TOM HULL, TYLER JOHNSON
PRODUCERS: KID HARPOON, TYLER JOHNSON
ALTERNATE VERSIONS: RADIO 1 LIVE LOUNGE, *ONE NIGHT ONLY IN NEW YORK*

DAYLIGHT

This summery synthpopper generated a great deal of speculation among fans because Taylor Swift – yes, her again – had included an identically-titled song on her 2019 album *Lover*. Obviously, that meant Harry's "Daylight" was an answer song.

Never mind that he was happily involved with actress/director Olivia Wilde at that point – what could the song be about other than a fleeting relationship that had ended nearly 10 years before?

Presenter Howard Stern tackled the subject directly when Harry was a guest on his SiriusXM show on May 18.

Stern asked if it was about a particular woman, and Styles reluctantly agreed, "Uh ... yeah." A woman "who didn't pay attention to you"? Could it be Taylor? "You're reading too much into it," Styles replied. "You know I'd love to tell you that you're spot-on, but you're not." Casting about for a vague-enough way to explain the song, he settled for "Our infatuation [with] chasing troubled things... is probably what 'Daylight's about."

He had a valid reason for not wanting to go into detail: in the song's first verse, the woman is using cocaine at his house, and if Styles had identified her, to Stern or any other interviewer, there could have been repercussions for her. (Perhaps intentionally, he slurs the word "cocaine", making it difficult to understand what he's saying.) "We will always wonder [about who she is]," Styles added enigmatically.

"Daylight" was among the first tranche of songs to be written for *Harry's House*. It was, as Styles said, about an infatuation with a woman who couldn't be present for him. "It's important to write from whatever you're going through at the time," he told Stern.

"Daylight" was the result of Styles, Hull and Johnson working through the night. They'd already been in the studio for most of the day, but once they began work on "Daylight", they felt compelled to push through for as long as it took to finish it. The work was going so magically well that they knew they couldn't go to bed before it was done; if they did, and then returned to it in the morning, it would be half the song it could have been. When it was done, they went to the beach and watched the sun come up.

Coincidentally, the video for "Daylight", with its travelling-circus storyline (Harry is part of a knife-throwing act, and gets shot out of a cannon) was the last *Harry's House* video to be released, on July 19, 2023, marking the end of the *HH* album era. In it, Styles also rides a horse for the first time in his life. "We told him, 'Just look like you're confident'," a rep from the Stampede Stunt Company told BBC Three Counties Radio.

Opposite: Closing Radio 1's Big Weekend 2022 at War Memorial Park. Coventry, May 29, 2022.

Overleaf: Having a joyous time with Lizzo at Coachella, April 22, 2022.

ALBUM TRACK

LITTLE FREAK

RELEASED: MAY 20, 2022
WRITERS: HARRY STYLES, TOM HULL
PRODUCERS: KID HARPOON, TYLER JOHNSON
ALTERNATE VERSION: *ONE NIGHT ONLY IN NEW YORK*

Despite the ribald connotations of "freak" – in the US especially, it refers to a sexually uninhibited woman – "Little Freak" is a soft, pensive look back at a relationship that didn't quite work out.

From the lyric, it's evident that Styles was hoping for more than the other person could give; but as he recounts little things he remembers about their time together – her athleisure wear, her scraped-back hair, the yoga-honed figure he never got to see – he's sad, yet not distraught. He seems to have reached the "acceptance" stage of mourning their almost-relationship.

He reviews his behaviour in the early stages, admitting he fell too hard for her when she didn't reciprocate his feelings, and he ruefully wishes that he'd at least been able to show her his birthmark. The implication there is that it's on a part of his body that she hadn't seen. (He has one on his right hand, and it's said that there's one on his back, but Harry hasn't posted any clues.) One of the prettiest things on the album, the soft-rock track was fittingly described by *Esquire* in May 2022 as a "cry-bop".

If things had gone to plan, "Little Freak" would have been on *Fine Line*, because it was written during the sessions for that album. It was early 2019 and Styles was in Tokyo, celebrating the New Year; he stayed in the city long enough to also mark his 25th birthday there on February 1. During that month, he invited Tom Hull to come out and write, and Hull proposed that when he got there, they hire guitars and a mic. "It was a vaguely disguised lads' trip," Hull told *Music Week* in March 2021 – could this have been the first time the time-tested "lads' trip" excuse was used as a cover-up for songwriting sessions?

They holed up with the guitars and the worst rental mic Styles had ever used, and came up with several songs (the *Harry's House* track "Boyfriends" was also conceived during those sessions, and also deemed not quite right for the vibe of *Fine Line*). Hull told *Rolling Stone* in September 2022 that "Little Freak" had been "produced and mixed in a whole different version for *Fine Line*, but it just didn't feel right". Hull finally returned to the track during the *HH* sessions, listened again to the wonky-mic sound of the demo and was inspired. Eric Alper, presenter of *That Eric Alper's Show* on SiriusXM, wrote about how the track was finally brought to life: "The intimate, raw feel of that initial, distorted Tokyo demo was so compelling that Johnson and Kid Harpoon decided to replicate it for the final album version using analog tape hiss and ambient room sounds."

Opposite: Fans waiting to get into the second night of Styles' *Love on Tour* Madison Square Garden residency. New York, August 21, 2022.

CHASE ENTRANCE
ADISON SQUARE GARDEN
THE WORLD'S MOST FAMOUS ARENA
BARK FOR US
woof woof
woof woof

LOVE ON TOUR
'22
HS

MATILDA

ALBUM TRACK

RELEASED: MAY 20, 2022
WRITERS: HARRY STYLES, TOM HULL, TYLER JOHNSON, AMY ALLEN
PRODUCERS: KID HARPOON, TYLER JOHNSON
ALTERNATE VERSION: *ONE NIGHT ONLY IN NEW YORK*

"There's this Harry Styles song that I co-wrote with him called 'Matilda'. It wasn't a big single, it wasn't all over the radio – it's a deep cut," said Amy Allen in an interview with CBS News in December 2025.

"But that is the song I get reached out to probably the most of any song I've ever been part of, in terms of resonating with people and really striking a chord with them. That makes me feel like everything I'm doing is worth it."

American songwriter-musician Allen has over 500 songs in her songwriting catalogue, including "Adore You" (for which she, Styles and the track's other writers won the 2021 Ivor Novello Award for Most Performed Work of 2020), but when asked by CBS "What are you most proud of when you hear a song you've written?" she instantly cited "Matilda".

Matilda Wormwood, main character in the Roald Dahl book *Matilda*, lent her name to this especially emotional song. Dahl's Matilda is the intellectually and telekinetically gifted daughter of emotionally abusive parents, and she uses her abilities to distance herself from them. Styles found the name fitting for the song he wrote about a young woman who'd confided in him about her own traumatic upbringing.

They didn't know each other well, but in the process of getting acquainted, she told him about early experiences that had left her emotionally compromised. In telling Styles, she seemed not to realize that she was even now affected by past abuse, but he recognized that she was still in pain, and recommended that she get help.

The naturally empathetic Styles is nothing if not a good listener, and to Matilda he provided non-judgemental sympathy. He also recognized that her family circumstances had given her the idea that emotional suffering was the norm. He hopes that the song, which he regarded as self-explanatory – one of the few in his catalogue that is – might have helped her to take the first step towards recovery. One of the positive things he derived from it was knowing that in making the song, he'd tried to support another person, which to him was as important – no, more important – than writing material for and about himself.

A soft pop-folk ballad, "Matilda" began life as "a great acoustic guitar part, and we wrote it around that," Tom Hull told *Sound on Sound* in January 2024. From that guitar part, it grew into what you could call a safe space for anyone who, like Matilda, grew up feeling unappreciated or less-than. A May 2022 *Nylon* track review singled out that quality as the song's strongest point: "Styles turns a singular experience into a comforting anthem that's applicable to anyone feeling out of step with their surroundings."

Opposite: Emphatically collared at the *Don't Worry Darling* red carpet at the Venice International Film Festival, September 5, 2022.

ALBUM TRACK

RELEASED: MAY 20, 2022
WRITERS: HARRY STYLES, SAMUEL WITTE
PRODUCERS: KID HARPOON, TYLER JOHNSON, SAMUEL WITTE
ALTERNATE VERSION: *ONE NIGHT ONLY IN NEW YORK*

CINEMA

Styles habitually declines to reveal who his songs are about, to the point of using the same ambiguous phrase every time he's asked. It goes like this: "Most of the time when I write songs, they start out as mine. It's important to write from whatever you're going through at the time."

That was his reply to Howard Stern when the SiriusXM presenter inquired about the background of "Cinema" during a May 2022 interview. Stern said, "You met your present girlfriend [when] she was directing you in a movie. And you are in love." As ever, Styles refused to confirm or deny.

Not to be fobbed off, Stern persisted, "You fell in love on a movie set?" Styles carefully replied, "I had a wonderful experience being directed by Olivia. Acting is very uncomfortable at times. I think you have to trust a lot." Stern played a brief excerpt from "Cinema", then put it to Harry that it was a love song. "It is," Styles agreed uncomfortably.

For once, he could hardly deny it. He'd met Olivia Wilde in September 2020 when she directed him in *Don't Worry Darling*, a creepy thriller that was his third film role. They hit it off – in a Styles cover story for the December 2020 issue of *American Vogue*, she said that she especially admired him for "redefining what it can mean to be a man with confidence". They were photographed holding hands, they kissed on an Italian yacht and in April 2022 he told SiriusXM's *Morning Mash Up* that he was "really happy at the moment".

Above: Cinema in action: Harry and *My Policeman* co-star Emma Corrin accept the TIFF Tribute Award at the Toronto International Film Festival, September 11, 2022.

Opposite: Facing the crowd at the *My Policeman* premiere. Toronto International Film Festival, September 11, 2022.

And so, "Cinema": a happy, sexy – all right, sexual – morsel of pop-funk that seems to have taken some of its sleek cues from George Michael's *Older* album era. When it was written, Harry had reached the loved-up stage of the relationship, where couples are simultaneously comfortable and hopelessly smitten. Thus, the lyric offers both tenderness and untrammelled lust, and also expresses a touch of likeable worry: was he coming on too strong? Would she be put off by his eagerness? He'd even tattooed her name on his right leg. Sadly, the relationship ended in late 2022.

He wrote the song over an extended period; as Styles told Apple Music around the time of the album's release, he was running on a treadmill when the chorus came to him, after which "I did a little [writing] here and then I went home and added a little bit there, and then kind of left it, and then went into the studio to put it all together."

The guitar solo was played by John Mayer, who'd once had such a crush on Wilde that in 2012 he wrote a song called "Something Like Olivia".

DAYDREAMING

ALBUM TRACK

RELEASED: MAY 20, 2022
WRITERS: HARRY STYLES, TOM HULL, TYLER JOHNSON
PRODUCERS: KID HARPOON, TYLER JOHNSON
ALTERNATE VERSION: *ONE NIGHT ONLY IN NEW YORK*

"Cinema" and "Daydreaming" make a lovely pair. Styles has rarely sounded as happy as he does on these album-mates, and to keep the "Cinema" momentum going, he even nudged John Mayer onto this track, too.

While "Daydreaming" shares "Cinema's" brimming-with-happiness feel, it's also a very different piece of music. It's built from a slice of disco and a big serving of '70s funk. To that end, it includes genuine '70s funk, in the form of a sample from the 1978 track "Ain't We Funkin' Now" by The Brothers Johnson. The sample, of a sinuous chant by female backing singers, plays a core role in "Daydreaming" – it drives the song along in the first minute, and again at the end of each verse. Styles's own backing vocalists, India Boodram and Alayna Rodgers, angelically sing the verses with him, building the track into a delightfully airy confection.

And then there's Harry's vocal performance, which finds him in the zone as never before. We knew he could produce a decent falsetto when called upon, but who had any idea that he could whoop and scream? He melds with the sample so seamlessly that he could be part of the original recording. In March 2026, *Rolling Stone* ranked it the 43rd-best of all his songs, commenting, "... feels like it was made for remixing into a late-night party jam at least four times its original three-minute length".

Lyrically, things are kept simple. Harry is about to leave for a long period – touring? Recording? We don't know – and wants a memory to sustain him while he's away – something to daydream about.

He provided an insight into the making of the song at a May 22 arena show called *One Night Only in New York*, where he performed *Harry's House* in its entirety.

"Before we play the next song ['Daydreaming'], another thank you to my good friend and producer Tyler Johnson," he told the crowd. "Tyler first sent me a voicenote for this song when I was driving from Palm Springs to LA. I think it was called Idea on the 101 Rough. It's no longer called that, thank God, but I haven't stopped singing it since."

He and Mayer have maintained their friendship, by the way. On January 23, 2026, Mayer hosted him on his SiriusXM show, *Life with John Mayer*. The guitarist proved an engaged interviewer. His first question touched on the length of Style's new single, "Aperture", which had been released that day; was its 5.11-minute running time an act of defiance against "some law of cultural physics"? Not really, said Styles; he'd experimented with removing certain sections, but in the end decided the longer version was "the best version of the song". An interesting insight into Styles' songwriting process.

Opposite: Doing his bit at a *Don't Worry Darling* photo call at AMC Lincoln Square Theater. New York, September 19, 2022.

IMAX
LIVE
AMERICAN EXPRESS
PLATINUM
Worry

KEEP DRIVING

ALBUM TRACK

RELEASED: MAY 20, 2022
WRITERS: HARRY STYLES, TOM HULL, TYLER JOHNSON, MITCH ROWLAND
PRODUCERS: KID HARPOON, TYLER JOHNSON
ALTERNATE VERSION: *ONE NIGHT ONLY IN NEW YORK*

Harry has never said that he intended "Cinema", "Daydreaming" and "Keep Driving" to be heard as a trilogy, but they do fit together. The first two take us through a day of smoochy bliss followed by a night of funkin', and "Keep Driving" sees us into the morning after, when the only thing on Harry's mind is food.

At first, all is well: he muses about swimming, lounging in the sun and snapping black-and-white pictures, and it's clear that life is pretty dandy. Then, over a cooked breakfast – coffee, eggs and the rest – he starts to cogitate over his relationship with the other person in the room (we know she's there because he's made two servings of pancakes). Styles' lyrics have often alluded to romantic uncertainty, and that's what they do here: does the girl he loves feel the same?

As an escape from troublesome thoughts, should they just get in the car and drive? And keep driving despite a niggling worry about a noise from the engine ("engine" being a metaphor for "relationship")? Once again, Styles has embedded these thoughts into a misleadingly bubbly, '70s-style synth arrangement – if you didn't listen to the words, you'd think it was one of the album's most optimistic songs. Aptly, the track would make great driving music, especially with the top down and an empty highway ahead.

But then Styles reaches the song's bridge and last verse, and an arresting stream-of-consciousness flow follows. Should they go on holiday? Oh, there are their passports, on the floor of the car. And there are some drugs, maybe: "edibles" and "puff" point that way, as well as a naked reference to cocaine. Oh, someone has a toothache. Let's have more coffee. I can see sideboob. There's a cyborg. There's a riot in America (this might refer to the Black Lives Matter protests that erupted after the police killing of George Floyd in May 2020 – Styles attended a Los Angeles protest on June 4). It's troubled and troubling, but maybe the underlying message is one of resilience – just keep going.

He hasn't spoken much about this song, apart from a comment after he played it at a show at Brixton Academy, South London, on May 24. It was one of two gigs titled *One Night Only* – the other had been in New York four days earlier – and because the Academy's capacity was just 5,000, demand for tickets was impossibly high. The £50 tickets went in minutes; immediately afterwards, they appeared on resale sites for up to £1,500. "I never thought I would say cocaine with my mother in the room," Styles said, and the crowd turned as one to wave at mum Anne sitting in the balcony.

Opposite: Poster and scenes from Styles' 2022 thriller *Don't Worry Darling*, co-starring Florence Pugh.

FLORENCE PUGH
HARRY STYLES
OLIVIA WILDE
GEMMA CHAN
KIKI LAYNE
NICK KROLL
AND CHRIS PINE
are you ready to live the life you deserve?
OLIVIA WILDE
Don't Worry Darling
only in theaters
SEPTEMBER 23
Dolby Cinema
NEW LINE CINEMA
R
CAREY VAN DYKE & SHANE VAN DYKE AND KATIE SILBERMAN
KATIE SILBERMAN
OLIVIA WILDE
WARNER BROS.

SATELLITE

SINGLE

RELEASED: MAY 3, 2023 (SINGLE) / MAY 20, 2022 (ALBUM)
WRITERS: HARRY STYLES, TOM HULL, TYLER JOHNSON
PRODUCERS: KID HARPOON, TYLER JOHNSON
ALTERNATE VERSION: *ONE NIGHT ONLY IN NEW YORK*

"NASA began a historic voyage to Mars with the Nov. 26, 2011, launch of the Mars Science Laboratory, which carries a car-sized rover named *Curiosity*," says the official NASA site.

Footage of the countdown and the rocket lifting off from the Kennedy Space Center, in Florida, is included. Years later, the rover is still operating, sending back pictures from the surface of Mars.

The launch is shown in the "Satellite" video – Styles is backstage at a venue, preparing for a show, and a screen above the musicians-and-crew buffet table is tuned to the lift-off footage. But no one is watching except a robot vacuum cleaner named Stomper.

Stomper stops hoovering the dressing room to observe the launch; then, his/her mind made up, he/she speeds out of the room and onto the stage, where Styles is performing this song. The poor vacuum is wrenched off the stage by security and leaves the venue to travel across America. It finally ends up in a field with Styles, where both watch the starry night sky as Stompy's battery runs down. The oddly touching video mirrors the narrative of this song, in which Styles watches a former love and compares himself to a satellite spinning in the sky, waiting for her to notice him and return to him.

The electropop song is perfectly listenable on its own, but the Aube Perrie-directed video adds to the pleasure of the experience. (The Paris-based filmmaker also directed the equally surreal "Music for a Sushi Restaurant" video.) *Business Insider*'s May 2022 track review said the song "gives the initial impression that it's going to be slow, sad, and spacious. But then he starts spinning up and out, crashing into little pockets of joy like they're bumpers in a game of pinball". That precisely captures the helium-stoked feel of the music, which whirls along in counterpoint to Styles' disconsolate lyric. We've all experienced the sensation of being far from home and the people we love. As for the nuts and bolts of his vocal performance, it's been praised by vocal coach Kaden Dayton: "It's light, but there is ... substance to it. The chorus is even lighter, even more in [his] head voice," he said in a May 8, 2023, post on his *YouTube* channel.

Dayton's assessment appeared five days after "Satellite" was released as the album's fourth single. *Harry's House* had been out for three weeks short of a year then, and, sadly, the single met the same chart fate as the last singles from *Fine Line* – it managed a No. 18 placing in Britain, and No. 21 in America. By the time an LP has been available for a year, anyone who wants to stream or download a track will have done it.

Opposite: Performing at the Grammy Awards at the crypto.com Arena, Los Angeles, on February 5, 2023.

Overleaf: Accepting one of two Grammys (Album of the Year and Best Pop Vocal Album) he won at the 2023 Awards.

BOYFRIENDS

ALBUM TRACK

RELEASED: MAY 20, 2022
WRITERS: HARRY STYLES, TOM HULL, TYLER JOHNSON, TOBIAS JESSO JR.
PRODUCERS: KID HARPOON, TYLER JOHNSON
ALTERNATE VERSIONS: *ONE NIGHT ONLY IN NEW YORK*, ACOUSTIC VERSION ON JAPANESE SHOW *THE FIRST TAKE*

The Yiddish word "mensch" – "a person of integrity" – fits Styles. His decency and insistence on doing the right thing have been praised many times, by those who know him and those who don't.

During his relationship with Olivia Wilde, she told *Vogue* in November 2020 that he was "devoid of toxic masculinity", while a superfan, Hannah Condon, told *The Guardian* in September 2022, "Harry never seems to do anything in half measures; his good deeds are plentiful and always seem organic."

Which brings us to "Boyfriends". Styles attributes his core values to having a sister, Gemma, three years his elder, and seeing her with her boyfriends. Well before he himself was old enough to be anyone's boyfriend, he observed that not all of her dates treated her well, and the same held true for many of her female friends. And he's never stopped worrying about her: at a September 2015 One Direction show in London, he told the audience, "I'm sorry if I seem distracted. My sister's here on a date, and I'm trying to keep an eye on it."

A nightmare scenario for Gemma and her date, but typical of Styles' protectiveness and high regard for women. A concomitant low regard for men was exhibited when he played "Boyfriends" live for the first time at Coachella on April 15, 2022: bringing his mainly-female band to the front of the stage, he introduced the song with "To boyfriends everywhere: f*** you!"

That's pretty much what this soft-spoken folk ballad does: it metaphorically badmouths bad boyfriends. The entire lyric amounts to a lecture from a concerned brother or a best friend, who sees the damage a toxic relationship is causing. The guy doesn't appreciate his woman, belittles her, drinks on the quiet and only phones when there's nothing better on the horizon. And the woman is a fool to put up with it – the lyric gently chides her for returning to a damaging man.

It was written at the end of the *Fine Line* sessions; the album was more or less done, but he had an extra week of studio time, so he made a rough demo. Canadian songwriter Tobias Jesso Jr. was there, and he played some chords for Styles. The next day, Styles requested "those chords you were playing", after which Jesso heard nothing for two years. Then a message from Harry: he'd used the chords, changing them to suit the song, and just wanted to let Jesso know. An impressed Jesso told *Rolling Stone*, "It's a rare thing to have somebody like Harry take the time to reach out to a songwriter after two years." Quite a mensch.

Opposite: Opening the 2023 Brit Awards with 2022's global and UK top-selling single, "As it Was". O2 Arena, London, February 11, 2023.

LOVE OF MY LIFE

ALBUM TRACK

RELEASED: MAY 20, 2022
WRITERS: HARRY STYLES, TOM HULL, TYLER JOHNSON
PRODUCERS: KID HARPOON, TYLER JOHNSON
ALTERNATE VERSION: *ONE NIGHT ONLY IN NEW YORK*

This song, and its place in the tracklist as the album's closing number, occasioned a storm of guesses about the who and the why of it. The "why" was easily explained: if the loose theme of *Harry's House* was "home", this sparse, deeply intimate song felt like a place to come home to.

After the clamour of the preceding songs – "Matilda"'s trauma, say, and "Keep Driving"'s sex and drugs – "Love of My Life" is the moment the album takes a deep breath, exhales and drops onto the sofa. There's so little to it other than a piano, a bit of guitar and Harry's tender vocal. The end.

The "who" of it excited great speculation; depending on who was guessing, it was supposedly either a former girlfriend, or Louis Tomlinson. The lyric was giving nothing away: there was a passing reference to checking into hotels under a pseudonym, and to being with a friend called Jonny. The latter was later revealed as his childhood friend Jonathan Harvey – at a June 2024 show in Dublin, Styles dedicated "Love of My Life" to "Jonny", who was in the audience, and revealed, "He is *the* Jonny from the song."

A sector of the fandom who call themselves Larries have long claimed that Styles and Tomlinson, or "Larry Stylinson", to use the official fandom name, have been in a romantic relationship since the early days of One Direction. Videos exist purporting to show definitive evidence: one Larry compiled a TikTok reel of Louis and Harry wearing (at different times) similar England football shirts. What gives it away on *Harry's House*, it seems, is the order of the songs; played in reverse order, starting with "Love of My Life", a timeline of their relationship apparently unfolds.

On another tack entirely, there would be more social-media fizzing in 2024, when Taylor Swift included a song called "LOML" on *The Tortured Poets Department.* Surely it had to be about Harry rather than her most recent ex, Matty Healy?!

The much less exciting truth? It's about England, and his unambiguous, unembarrassed love of home. He'd always wanted to address the subject in a song, but was worried that it would lapse into cliché – how would he do it without singing about the pub and the chippy?

The solution was to strip it back to bare bones – so bare that the recording of it was terrifying. At first, he was unsure it would work. His bedroom was over the studio, and as he listened to it repeatedly being played downstairs he was riven by doubt. Tom Hull and Tyler Johnson, though, loved it and persuaded him to finish it. And he loves it himself now.

Opposite above: Styles won in four categories at the 2023 Brit Awards: Artist, Album, Song and Pop/R&B Act.

Opposite below: Styles accepts the statuette for Artist of the Year at the 2023 Brit Awards. O2 Arena, London, February 11, 2023.

DUETS AND COLLABORATIONS

Harry has yet to fully collaborate with another artist on record. While other musicians *have* appeared on his albums, their role has been confined to backing vocals (Wolf Alice's Ellie Rowsell added her voice to "Aperture", "Taste Back" and "Season 2 Weight Loss" on *Kiss All the Time. Disco, Occasionally.*) or playing guitar (as John Mayer and Ben Harper did on *Harry's House*). Initially, it was probably a deliberate strategy: he had to prove he could go it alone, which would be undermined if he shared a track with a big-name featured vocalist on his first couple of albums. Now that his artistic credentials have been established, though, it won't be surprising if there's a "Harry Styles feat" credit in his future.

But duets? Another thing entirely. He's done plenty, including a team-up with Rowsell in Lisbon on July 31, 2022 – the last European date of his *Love on Tour* trek. Wolf Alice had opened for Styles on the European leg, and Styles extended his thanks by singing joint lead vocals on Wolf Alice's "No Hard Feelings" during his encore. For someone who started as a pop singer, he adapted himself to the group's gritty alt-rock as if he'd sung it all his life.

Then there was a duet that was viewed by fans as a landmark moment: Shania Twain and Styles on the first weekend of his 2022 Coachella headliner, where they sang Twain's "You're Still the One" and "Man! I Feel Like a Woman". The country star, who later supported Styles at his 2026 Wembley Stadium shows in London, is something of an icon to Harry fans, who heard her music when they were growing up. Together at Coachella, they were magical. (Twain said it was one of the highlights of her career.) It didn't hurt that they wore matching sequined costumes.

The second Coachella weekend brought an even more memorable meet-up. For Lizzo-fan Styles, what could have been more glorious than singing the disco perennial "I Will Survive" in matching feathered coats (pink-and-white for him, orange for her)? The answer had to be: singing One Direction's "What Makes You Beautiful" with her. And when he repaid the compliment, appearing at a Lizzo show in Miami Beach in 2020 to duet "Juice", the two produced the purest expression of joy you'll ever see on a concert stage.

Stevie Nicks has been a friend since he presented her with a carrot cake at a Fleetwood Mac show in 2015, and the two have guested at each other's shows. Nicks was there at Harry's gig at the Troubadour in Los Angeles in May 2017, when they sang his "Two Ghosts" and her "Landslide" and "Leather and Lace" (as Styles prepared to join in on "Landslide", he looked decidedly nervous, knowing he was in the presence of a certified icon). On July 12, 2024, less nervous now, he appeared during the encore of her own show in London's Hyde Park. They sang her solo hit "Stop Draggin' My Heart Around" and the Mac track "Landslide", the latter dedicated to the late Christine McVie, whose 81st birthday it would have been.

Styles tends to duet with women, but there have been intriguing link-ups with male artists, too. The best, arguably, was with Stormzy. Precisely nobody expected the rapper to pop into Styles' December 2019 gig at London's Electric Ballroom and perform his recent UK No. 1, "Vossi Bop"; the audience reacted with near-hysteria as he and Styles traded ad-libs. At the end, a jubilant Stormzy said, "Harry Styles is a f***ing legend... from my heart, bro, you're not just a pop star, you're a brilliant artist."

Opposite: With Shania Twain at Coachella, April 15, 2022. The combined wattage of their outfits could have powered a city.

KISS ALL THE TIME. DISCO, OCCASIONALLY.

In which Harry visits the Berlin superclub Berghain and makes a dance record. Well, almost. Though he recorded part of his fourth album at Berlin's celebrated Hansa Studios, where he leaned into electronic sounds, and he did shake a leg at Berghain, he also found space for disco, funk and soft balladry. The nearly four years between *Harry's House* and *Kiss All the Time. Disco, Occasionally*. were consumed by touring, turning 30 and living in Italy, where he reassessed his life and career. *The Times*' review picked up on that: "This feels like the product of a bunch of people making music together and enjoying it."

APERTURE

SINGLE

RELEASED: JANUARY 22, 2026 (SINGLE) / MARCH 6, 2026 (ALBUM)
WRITERS: HARRY STYLES, TOM HULL
PRODUCER: KID HARPOON
ALTERNATE VERSIONS: LIVE AT 2026 BRIT AWARDS, *ONE NIGHT ONLY IN MANCHESTER*

Styles went to the Berlin techno club Berghain the night before he made the song that would be *Kiss All the Time*'s first track, first single and first No. 1.

He didn't sleep much between getting home from the club and making his way to the studio. "I was tired," he told Apple Music's Zane Lowe during an interview on March 4, 2026, two days ahead of the album's release. Tiredness can work in mysterious ways: "I think it ended up being the freest song on the record."

The word "aperture" means "opening" – most commonly the opening that allows light to enter a camera. Styles interpreted it as "giving yourself the space to let light in," he told Lowe. More specifically, the song was about realizing that he'd been wrong about an unspecified issue. He elaborated, "You can move forward when you acknowledge things that you don't know" – and from that comes enlightenment, letting light in. "It's why I think 'Aperture' felt like the perfect start to me."

The "perfect start" was actually the last song made for the album, but Styles saw it as the record's "mission statement," he told Radio 2 the day after the single's release. It feels like it was created as such: five minutes of house piano and an LCD Soundsystem-adjacent euphoric rise and fall, before it all subsides with a kind of sigh, as if to signal "mission accomplished". As ever in his lyric-writing, Styles hasn't pinpointed exactly what he means – the track's verses and chorus plant a hazy idea of fighting back against something, possibly the temptation to drink, because he alludes to sobriety. He cautiously accepts a new situation, which could be a romantic one, and commits to letting in the light.

"... allowing for more things, and internaliz[ing] the more positive things to come into your life was a lot about what this song and this album as a whole was about for me," he told Radio 2. "And also the openness to be accepting of transitions and flaws and your own mistakes." (Styles has seen a therapist since around 2017, he told *Better Homes & Gardens* during a 2022 interview. He's found that therapy "opens up rooms in myself", and he's progressed to the point of accepting himself as he is. Therapy has shifted his world-view, which can be perceived in his explanation of "Aperture". His therapist gets an actual mention on "Are You Listening Yet?".)

On its first day, "Aperture" was streamed 12.4 million times on Spotify; by February 27, it had reached 100 million. Not bad for a tune he described to Radio 1's Greg James as "a perfect little bow" – that's "bow" meaning a ribbon attached to a gift.

Opposite: At the 2026 Grammys, where he presented Bad Bunny with the Album of the Year award. February 1, 2026.

AMERICAN GIRLS

SINGLE

RELEASED: MARCH 6, 2026 (SINGLE AND ALBUM)
WRITERS: HARRY STYLES, TOM HULL, TYLER JOHNSON
PRODUCERS: KID HARPOON, TYLER JOHNSON
ALTERNATE VERSIONS: RADIO 1 LIVE LOUNGE, *ONE NIGHT ONLY IN MANCHESTER*

Styles' core desire is similar to most other people's: he wants someone to love, and a family. "American Girls" takes on that subject – an increasingly "lonely" one for him because as an unmarried man in his thirties (though he's been dating Zoe Kravitz since 2025), he's starting to find himself the odd one out among his friends. He told Zane Lowe in March 2026 that the track is "quite a lonely song in a lot of ways", and the lyric confirms it.

This is one of the rare occasions when a Styles lyric doesn't need much deciphering – well, more or less. The meanings of a few typically Stylesian couplets in the first and second verses will be obvious to the friends he wrote them about, but perhaps not to others. As a *Vulture* reviewer wrote in March 2026, he "errs on the side of vagueposting". (Though a picture does emerge when he sings words like "temptations" and "frustrations".)

As for the rest, his feelings couldn't be clearer. His friends have found happiness with American women and Harry is wrestling with the idea that they've made these commitments. There's a touch of jealousy as he acknowledges that they're in love and have chosen to be with their other halves for better, for worse, for richer, for poorer.

"I watched my three closest friends get married," he told Lowe. "Actually seeing them trust in something and risk something to find something truly fulfilling..." impelled him to look at his own life. At first, he reminded himself that he was the carefree bachelor of the crew, so he was "having all the fun", but that didn't wash for long. The more he thought about what his mates had "risked" by marrying – because "it doesn't come without any uncertainty, it doesn't come without any risk" – the more he saw the risk as one worth taking.

"I want to be in great relationships with people," he said. "I want a family. I want these things." More than that, he wants a partner who understands his desire to be the best person he can be, and who will call him out if he doesn't live up to his own standards. "I think accepting flaws and stuff is wonderful, but, you know, I want to be better than that, so when you challenge me on something, it's a gift to me."

"American Girls" turns into the album's rock(ish) song when it hits its big, Van Halenesque chorus, but many reviewers considered it one of the slighter tracks on *Kiss All the Time.*; the *NME*, for instance, deemed it pleasant but "easily forgettable".

Did Harry care? The single reached No. 1 in the same week that the album did, so he's probably not bothered.

Opposite above: A Los Angeles billboard advertises Styles' *One Night in Manchester* show, streamed on Netflix on March 8, 2026.

Opposite below: A teaser poster – seen here in London, January 14, 2026 – that appeared just before the release of "Aperture".

HARRY
LIKES IT WHEN
YOU WATCH

paloma—wool
7-8 Conduit St, LONDON
WE BELONG TOGETHER

Styles is decades too young to have watched *Ready Steady Go!*, the Friday-night British music programme that ran from 1963 to 1966. (Note the absence of commas in its name – those who appreciate accurate punctuation must be pleased by their inclusion in the song title.)

The show fully merits the overused adjective "iconic" for its informal presentation of the era's biggest bands, and for serving as a guide to the Swinging London cultural scene.

Despite having been born in 1994, Styles is a pop-culture vulture who has spent a good part of his solo career acquainting himself with the music and pop ephemera that have gone before. See also the song's official lyric video, with its black-and-white graphic that resembles the title card of a '60s TV show (the album's other lyric videos use the same artwork).

But he's been running marathons, too, completing the Tokyo and Berlin races in under 3:25, and the song title might also pertain to the runners' phrase "ready, steady, go". Harry's not saying, and the song tells us little beyond the fact (maybe) that he's strongly attracted to a woman who makes him feel fluttery and nervous. The term "ready, steady, go", repeated 25 times, plus once – "*pronti, quasi, vai!*" – in Italian, seems to be his flinging caution to the wind and diving into something physical. (Using Italian undoubtedly relates to happy memories of a sojourn in Rome in 2024, where he now owns a house in a village in the centre of the country near his friend, fashion designer Alessandro Michele, and has spent much of his time in recent years.)

Yet the music itself, gently bassy and whooshy
feel of an after-the-club comedown song rather
seduction number. And there's a musical wildcar
at 2.06 minutes: a brief, keyboard-tinkling allusio
Fears' 1983 hit "Change". Through therapy, has S
to appreciate growth and change ... or is that re
into this song?

Safeguarding his mystique has been one of his
throughout his career, so it's unlikely that he'll e
the song means. He simply allows fans and critic
they will. The name Leon comes up in the chorus,
"calling" him – again, what was in his mind? Fans
that Leon is Leonard "Lenny" Kravitz, father of gi

Critical response to "Ready, Steady, Go!" has b
It's "an undeniable banger", according to *Vulture*
album review, and *Rolling Stone* also found it "a t
Hollywood Reporter agreed: "It's catchy enough
likely find themselves singing the chorus back to
The Guardian, meanwhile, admiringly likened its
experiments" to "a sleeker version of [American
The Rapture."

Opposite: Giving "Aperture" the full song-and-dance treatment at the Brit Awards. Co-op Live, Manchester, February 28, 2026.

ARE YOU LISTENING YET?

ALBUM TRACK

RELEASED: MARCH 6, 2026
WRITERS: HARRY STYLES, TOM HULL, TYLER JOHNSON
PRODUCERS: KID HARPOON, TYLER JOHNSON
ALTERNATE VERSION: *ONE NIGHT ONLY IN MANCHESTER*

As mentioned in the "Aperture" entry (see page 192), Styles' therapist is shouted out on "Are You Listening Yet?". She turns up in the very first line of this disco-punk tune, introduced to the world, in a manner of speaking, by his sung-rapped declaration that she's doing pretty well out of him.

In other words, he finds her indispensable and, we're led to believe, he consults her frequently, including while on tour. We can also glean from his uncharacteristically rapid delivery, where words tumble over words, that he felt buoyed-up by the subject.

To infer from his interview with Zane Lowe in March 2026, "Are You Listening Yet?" was indeed informed by his experience of therapy. Explaining the genesis of *Kiss All the Time.*, he's frequently said that taking a two-year break after his 169-date *Love on Tour* marathon ended in July 2023 induced a great deal of soul-searching. "I wanted to make sure I still loved [making music]. It's a good thing, when you've done something for a long time, to stop and check in with yourself: do I do this because this is what I've done for a long time, or do I still love it?"

"Checking in" is a therapeutic term that refers to an assessment of one's emotional well-being. He told Lowe that doing so helped him to "take responsibility for places in my life where it was maybe my fault what happened – and that used to feel like such a scary place to delve into. I think being able to do that just freed me from so much. When you live in a way that's denying that stuff, you're living in the shadows."

"Are You Listening Yet?" is a direct meditation on taking responsibility, and on listening to your gut. It's the "oldest" song on the album – not necessarily the first written, but the oldest to make it onto the record. He was playing New York, which dates it to October 2021, and was "so in[to] it", and feeling "thrashy". The song, he said, came as a reaction to that feeling. There *is* a thrashiness to its clattering drums and urgent backing vocals from the House Gospel Choir. Most of all, there's a thrashiness to Styles' jittery vocal, which evokes James Murphy of LCD Soundsystem – a big favourite of Styles' – singing "Daft Punk is Playing at My House". (*The Guardian* felt he was closer to Robbie Williams on his hit "Rock DJ".)

The main point is that Styles isn't at ease with himself on the song. That, though, is all part of the therapeutic process. "I like the end refrain: 'Are you listening yet?' over and over again. By the time you *are* listening it's finished."

Opposite: Styles arrives at the 2026 Brit Awards in Manchester – the first time the Brits were held outside London.

Overleaf: Focusing on something only he can see? Brit Awards, Co-op Live, Manchester, February 28, 2026.

TASTE BACK

ALBUM TRACK

RELEASED: MARCH 6, 2026
WRITERS: HARRY STYLES, TOM HULL, TYLER JOHNSON
PRODUCERS: KID HARPOON, TYLER JOHNSON
ALTERNATE VERSION: *ONE NIGHT ONLY IN MANCHESTER*

Ellie Rowsell of the London band Wolf Alice contributes backing vocals to this mid-album deep cut (as she also does on "Aperture" and "Season 2 Weight Loss"), but she's so far down in the mix as to be just a gauzy presence harmonizing with Harry's lead vocal.

As she told the Press Association on the red carpet at the 2026 Brit Awards, where Wolf Alice won Group of the Year, "I'm not really featured, I just did some backing vocals."

In this case, though, that was exactly what was required: "Taste Back" is itself a hazy presence on the album, apart from its surging chorus. With admirable exactitude, *The Guardian* described the track as "subtly lit".

"Hazy" and "gauzy" are also watchwords for *Kiss All the Time.* itself. Styles told Zane Lowe in their March interview that his driving force while making the record was the question "How do I still have my experience while I'm playing it?" He formulated it on a night out: "I went to see Radiohead in Berlin, and felt so part of the audience. I'm watching this and feeling everything that's happening around me in the crowd." It was little short of an epiphany, endowing him with a sense of purpose different from what he'd known. "I had a moment of [thinking], 'I'm there so that people can have this. I'm soundtracking this.'"

To put it another way: "What music do I have to make for me to be on stage feeling like I'm in the middle of the dance floor?" One answer is "Taste Back": it's synth-washed and dreamy, yet propulsive enough to make audiences dance. When he sings it live, he's doing what he hoped to do; he's the soundtrack to the crowd's experience.

The track is about a relationship, or perhaps "situationship" is more accurate, because the lyric suggests that Styles is unsure how he feels about someone from the past who has just resurfaced. She phones him from Paris and addresses him as "baby", and it's evident to him that she must be lonely. He doesn't make it easy for her, asking how she has the nerve to use an endearment ("baby") and sardonically inquiring whether her taste has returned, as in, can this woman now appreciate what they had? There's an allusion – "white" – to either cocaine or wine, something that made her difficult to handle in the past. How will this end? Styles doesn't know.

Ellie Rowsell, meanwhile, has told *Marie Claire* about working with Styles: "I love singing harmonies, and I love Harry, so I was excited to sing on those tracks. Harry has a huge range vocally. I was really impressed by his placement of harmonies and stuff, I just copied what he'd already done."

Opposite: Giving his microphone a telling-off, apparently, at the 2026 Brit Awards.

THE WAITING GAME

ALBUM TRACK

RELEASED: MARCH 6, 2026
WRITERS: HARRY STYLES, TOM HULL, TYLER JOHNSON
PRODUCERS: KID HARPOON, TYLER JOHNSON
ALTERNATE VERSION: *ONE NIGHT ONLY IN MANCHESTER*

This fascinating tune reflects Styles' emotional progress during his post-*Love on Tour* two-year lay-off. He wrote "The Waiting Game" in the summer of 2024, while living in Italy, a country that has assumed great importance to him.

His stay there was "transitional", he told *The Sunday Times Magazine* in March.

It was the first time in years, probably since before he joined One Direction, that he'd spent longer than a few weeks in one place. "I remember going to a café [in Rome] and sitting and having a coffee and thinking, 'I don't remember the last time I sat down and had a coffee – if I've ever sat down and just had a coffee.'"

He'd spent the previous fourteen years living at such a frenetic pace that when he finally sat down and had that coffee in a city that puts a high value on living in the moment, he was profoundly affected. "The Romans are the best at that," he said. "That's their speciality. The pace they've taught me has been so special." His gratitude for his new way of living was heightened by his sister Gemma having had a baby around that time, which ignited a determination to be there while his new niece was growing up.

After he'd been in Italy for a while and felt settled, he was moved to write a song. "The Waiting Game", a whizzy electropop item with percussion that *Rolling Stone* compared to "Mavis Beacon" (a fictional character invented to help '80s computer users learn touch typing), came out of it. He was, he told Zan that zone of reflection," and the scales had fallen Essentially, the song was a note-to-self about the living with integrity, and while it was sung to a "y makes it plain that "you" means "I". (Obviously, th many fans from hitting social media with guesse was, with Taylor Swift being the main suspect.)

Styles told Lowe, "I just liked being that honest what I was doing, with music, with my life, with m and with cycles I'd got into. And... you always just waiting game." The waiting game is the passivene most – all? – of us when we've acknowledged the but haven't got around to changing.

Clash called the song "[a] self-analytical lyric s thoughts outside the therapist's office..." and the out. Styles is unsparing about what he considers he tells himself he romanticizes flaws, he doesn't he has agency (freedom to act), he apologizes wit How many pop stars can claim to be this honest?

Opposite: Styles and 25 dancers give "Aperture" its first live performance. Brit Awards, February 28, 2026.

PARLIAMENT

SEASON 2 WEIGHT LOSS

ALBUM TRACK

RELEASED: MARCH 6, 2026
WRITERS: HARRY STYLES, TOM HULL, TYLER JOHNSON
PRODUCER: KID HARPOON
ALTERNATE VERSION: *ONE NIGHT ONLY IN MANCHESTER*

A bee buzzes around the opening seconds of "Season 2 Weight Loss" – but it's a synthesizer rather than a bee, and the buzzing is followed by the crackle of computer circuitry.

After that, there's a humming, old-school synth line, and after *that* there are beats, which could be machine-made, or produced by Tom Skinner, a jazz drummer who appears on this track and five others.

All of this happens within the first 15 seconds of "Season 2 Weight Loss", and from there the song only gets more abstract. Styles' vocal, for one thing, is muffled and cloudy, and acts as a counterpoint to the battering breakbeats. If any track on *Kiss All the Time.* could be categorized as art-pop, it's this one.

More precisely, it's art-pop crossed with 21st-century pop culture. Styles was intrigued by the idea of artists becoming different "versions" of themselves when they become successful. In a March 2026 interview with Zane Lowe, he used a Netflix hit as an example. "You know when there's a Netflix show and then it blows up and everyone comes back in the second season? Everyone's got a nutritionist, and everyone's got a trainer, and everyone suddenly looks amazing? Season 2 weight loss."

His own version of season two germinated during his 2024–25 work hiatus. The resolution he made then to live more mindfully – basically, to take time to sit down and have a coffee – meant that the Styles who returned with *Kiss All the Time.* was "a stronger version of myself". That, though, came with a new worry. He used the analogy of growing a moustache whenever he gets a few weeks off – for him, it's the facial-hair equivalent of an out-of-office message. When it's time to go back to work, he shaves it off because he knows that a moustachioed Styles "isn't the version of me that people expect".

He applied the same version-of-himself quandary to the lyric of "Season 2 Weight Loss". Would the public accept an evolved pop star? "Will you take me as [the person he now was rather than his old self]?" he asked Lowe.

It's a knotty question and a knotty song. (He told Lowe that it's the album's "mission statement", though he's said the same about "Aperture".) Tom Hull told *The New York Times* it was never intended to be a Styles track; in its early stages, it was an experimental synth instrumental. But Styles loved the sound of it and they turned it into a song, albeit a song they didn't think would get onto the album. "There's a million moments where that song doesn't make the record. That's a song that slightly pushes the needle of what you can achieve."

Opposite: Styles collects band T-shirts – this one features Parliament's 1978 album, *Motor Booty Affair*. New York, March 11, 2026.

COMING UP ROSES

ALBUM TRACK

RELEASED: MARCH 6, 2026
WRITER: HARRY STYLES
PRODUCER: KID HARPOON
ALTERNATE VERSIONS: *SATURDAY NIGHT LIVE, ONE NIGHT ONLY IN MANCHESTER*

One day in December, Styles sat down to write a Christmas song. After two lines – which still exist, repurposed as the opening couplet to "Coming up Roses" – he thought better of it.

After considering it for a while, he realized that he hadn't really wanted to come up with a seasonal number; he just felt the need to do something different. With this track, he certainly has.

It marks several firsts: his debut as a solo songwriter, and his maiden voyage as a sleek crooner backed by a 39-piece orchestra. This crooner is, as ever, beset by doubts; here, he thinks he's found someone special, and wants to see where it goes. Even if the pair aren't destined for a long-term romance, he still sees value in a shorter-term connection. He told Zane Lowe that it's "about how special something can be, and not everything has to last forever in order for it to be special. Some of the greatest relationships in your life that teach you something don't last forever."

But the girlfriend is crying because he's conveyed the idea that he doesn't see permanence in their future. Right now, he's afraid she might believe that he didn't want her with him at all, when the opposite is true. He tries to reassure her as well as himself; the soundtrack to this fraught exchange is lush strings, plucked pizzicato. The delicate arrangement gives his voice centre stage; there are no competing beats or synth whorls on this track.

Despite their misunderstandings, though, he still believes that things could come up roses. The pair, after all, like and fancy each other, and given time perhaps their feelings can be brought into alignment – even permanently.

Styles said in spring 2026 that he'd like to have a family within five years, so it stands to reason that he brought a different criteria to his search for a partner during this period, and was no longer attracted to the idea of a brief fling. By the same token, however, he's not against a mad night together where the only thing that counts is having enough fun to wake up hungover in the morning.

He loves this song, but it might not have existed if Tom Hull hadn't chivvied him along. "I want to thank Tom for pushing me and believing in me to finish it and get it done," he said at the *One Night Only* show he staged at Manchester's Co-op Arena on March 6, 2026. "I've always struggled at times to believe in myself... I want to thank him for being the friend that he is to me. So, Tom, this one's for you."

Opposite: The sweatshirt pays tribute both to New York and the 1994 US Open tennis tournament. New York, March 24, 1996.

Overleaf: POV: how can they see with those sunglasses? Brit Awards, Co-op Live, Manchester, February 28, 2016.

New York
94

POP

ALBUM TRACK

RELEASED: MARCH 6, 2026
WRITERS: HARRY STYLES, TOM HULL, TYLER JOHNSON
PRODUCERS: KID HARPOON, TYLER JOHNSON
ALTERNATE VERSION: *ONE NIGHT ONLY IN MANCHESTER*

"I love pop music, and I think with this album, they're inherently pop songs," Styles explained to Radio 1's Jack Saunders on March 12, 2026, when he performed a Live Lounge set for the station. "I'm meant to be pop, it's supposed to be pop, and I think [the album is] playing with that. It's a very playful thing, pop music."

He's right about that. Pop is playful, but it can also be heartbreaking, profound or escapist, and Styles has expressed all of those impulses across *Kiss All the Time*. As for the song actually titled "Pop", it falls into the "playful" category. Constructed of the album's giddiest bassline – just try to stand still while listening; it's impossible – and funkiest keyboard hook, it's one of the record's most irresistible tracks.

Saying that, the lyric offers a darker, more complicated window into his private thoughts. The first two lines touch on drugs; he sings about "mainlining", and having run out of Rizlas, and if we take these lines at face value, he's referring to heroin and cannabis. That doesn't mean he uses either – the words are almost certainly intended as an analogy. They point to something raw and perhaps unresolved, a theory that's given credence by the rest of the verse.

Only someone who's been in a boy band can understand the oppressiveness of always having to be the boy next door – or, as Styles puts it here, "squeaky clean". (The most memorable instance of a boy band member deciding he wasn't going to take it any more was Robbie Williams' departure from Take That in 1995 – within a month, he'd appeared onstage with Oasis, been put in his place by Noel Gallagher – who called him "the fat dancer from Take That" – and seemed a most unlikely candidate for a decades-long run of No. 1 albums that he achieved.)

The word "pop" also refers to a sexual connection: when Styles gets "intimate" – a word he used on "Cinema" on *Harry's House* – with a woman, he "pops". That's "Styles' personal slang for *le petit mort*," *Rolling Stone* explained in March, noting that "Pop" was all about "the thrill of transgressing one's fresh-faced image". In a review the same month, *Dazed* hit on an identical meaning, contending that "Pop" describes "not only how the expectation to be polished has worn Styles down on the inside, but also how *Kiss All the Time.* paints outside of these lines".

The song was widely admired by the media. "… a superb, confident drum frenzy with another self-referential lyric" was *Classic Pop*'s judgement; *The Hollywood Reporter* declared it "a top-two contender for most fun you'll have", and *Billboard* got straight to the point with "A sure-footed strut around sex, drugs and dancing."

Opposite: A pop-up shop in Los Angeles celebrates the release of *Kiss All the Time. Disco, Occasionally.* March 6, 2026.

KISS KISS
KISS KISS
PRESENTED BY
AMERICAN EXPRESS
HARRY STYLES
SCION

DANCE NO MORE

ALBUM TRACK

RELEASED: MARCH 6, 2026
WRITERS: HARRY STYLES, TOM HULL
PRODUCER: KID HARPOON
ALTERNATE VERSIONS: RADIO 1 LIVE LOUNGE, *ONE NIGHT ONLY IN MANCHESTER*

"Dance No More" might not be – as *Variety*'s review put it – the album's "one true banger", because "Pop" is also on the record, and it bangs nearly as decisively.

But it might be the song that most embodies the revelation he had on the Berghain dancefloor in Berlin during his two-year break from touring

It was his first visit to Berghain, a club in a former power station that preserves its incredible hipness by enforcing a strict entry policy. *Time Out Berlin* summed it up in a few lines: "While there are no clear rules on how to get into Berghain, you should think about a few things before you join the sometimes-enormous queue. The biggest thing? Give respect and consideration to Berghain's culture and original intent: to provide a safe space for queer people to celebrate and indulge." Short shrift is given to people who come to stare. *Time Out* also suggests learning a few German phrases to communicate with the bouncers, who will look kindly on the effort. It's easy to imagine the polite and empathetic Styles doing just that.

The way he described it to Apple Music captured the fervour of a near-religious experience. He told Lowe about that first visit, during which he was "standing in the middle of the dance floor and feeling so unbelievably free and safe. I felt tears streaming down my face". To Radio 1's Jack Saunders, he elaborated, "I think anyone who's been in the middle of a dancefloor like that... I think knows that feeling of, 'I'm just covered in tears and sweat and it's all the same'."

That, we already know, gave him the impetus to make *Kiss All the Time.*, and "Dance No More" is his attempt to convert the visceral experience into a song. It starts with Styles taking a cautious look around the club; he's just arrived and tells his companion that he's uncomfortable – he doesn't know anyone and can't even get a bottle of water. But when he hears the music, he's knocked for six. The groove is funky, the jolts of synthesizer make him want to move, and the melody line is augmented by gang vocals – a group of people including Tom Hull shouting along with Styles.

He also manages to keep a promise he made to Fox Hull, son of Tom, in 2019. Styles namechecked Fox's mother, Jenny, on the *Fine Line* track "Canyon Moon", and Fox was jealous. How about a namecheck for *him*? Harry agreed – as long as he hit the crossbar during a football game he was about to play. Sure enough, there it is in the song's bridge: a clearly enunciated "Fox!"

Opposite: Fans outside Co-op Live, where Harry performed his *One Night in Manchester* show. March 6, 2026.

JUST TWO
AMERICAN GIRLS
HERE 4 HARRY

Harry Styles

PAINT BY NUMBERS

ALBUM TRACK

RELEASED: MARCH 6, 2026
WRITERS: HARRY STYLES, TOM HULL, TYLER JOHNSON
PRODUCERS: KID HARPOON, TYLER JOHNSON
ALTERNATE VERSION: *ONE NIGHT ONLY IN MANCHESTER*

The album's penultimate track is the simplest, most fuss-free 2.27 minutes on the record. It's as if, having spent the previous 10 songs discoing all the time, Styles needs a break from the dancefloor.

He sits down, a guitar is softly strummed and he gently works his way through a meditation on misperceptions about his life – every famous person learns to live with them – and how they've affected who he is. It's almost the first time on the album that we hear his voice unfiltered; its warmth is one of the pleasures of "Paint by Numbers".

Having been a public figure literally for half his life, Styles has had to navigate a course that has been complicated by the rise of social media. His generation of pop stars was the first to have its privacy invaded in real time; he could be sitting in a café in Rome and it would take just one person with a phone to broadcast his whereabouts around the world, usually attached to an unflattering photo. Luckily for Styles, he almost never takes a bad picture.

Adele, who achieved stardom at the same time as Harry in One Direction, told the German magazine *ZDF* in 2024, "I miss everything about before I was famous, I think probably being anonymous the most." Styles doesn't quite wish he was still working in a bakery in Holmes Chapel, but on "Paint by Numbers" he's frustrated by being an "image" that has little to do with his true self. He's perpetually perceived as being mystically different from ordinary humans, when he was just a guy who was lucky enough to have fulfilled a dream – in the song's first line, he calls success a "gift" – and he's smart enough to know that Megastar Harry is just a construct. "I love people, and I love being in the world," he said in a March interview with Canadian podcaster Tom Power. But he'd been learning to set boundaries, "and learning when not to set boundaries", and finding a balance.

The title "Paint by Numbers" documents that internal debate. Paint-by-numbers kits include an outline inside which users paint, and Styles sings about painting within the lines – trying to "be" the image the public thinks it sees – but invariably straying outside. "Like, you can try and paint inside the lines – but life just doesn't work that way," he told Power.

The track was originally slated to be the album opener, because "at that time the album was very different. It was very introspective". And despite ending up the next-to-last song instead, it remains introspective. There's a line about a relationship with an older person – Olivia Wilde? – but it otherwise simply tries to make sense of Harry's conflicting feelings.

Opposite: Kissing him all the time: fans outside a pop-up shop in Paris on album-release day. March 6, 2026.

CARLA'S SONG

ALBUM TRACK

RELEASED: MARCH 6, 2026
WRITERS: HARRY STYLES, TOM HULL
PRODUCER: KID HARPOON
ALTERNATE VERSIONS: RADIO 1 LIVE LOU

His insistence on keeping private things means that Styles avoids discussing his songs in any but the most general terms. The final track of *Kiss All the Time.*, though, is a different story.

He's been open about the exact circumstances that led to its creation – and has even identified Carla.

In a way, Carla was emblematic of the whole record; she represented the reason he'd made it. But who is she? She's a friend, part of his social circle, and one night, she was telling the group about a singer-songwriter she'd recently discovered; had any of them heard of Paul Simon?

Styles had. He'd lived in a pub when his mother and stepfather, Anne and John Cox, became landlords of the Antrobus Arms in Northwich, Cheshire, at the end of 2002; the pub PA system had a copy of the Simon & Garfunkel album *Bridge Over Troubled Water*. (The couple must have been popular – on April 9, 2003, the *Warrington Guardian* ran a story about their upcoming wedding at the Mere Golf Club.) So Harry was familiar with both Paul Simon's solo career – including the 1975 hit that Carla was "obsessively" listening to, "50 Ways to Leave Your Lover" – and the Simon & Garfunkel years.

He attributes his love of harmonies to endless exposure to *Bridge Over Troubled Water*, and, given Carla's "obsession" with "50 Ways", he told her she had to hear a song Simon recorded with Art Garfunkel. It was the album's majest
listen to it, having never heard that
someone see... something in Technic
There was something in that momen
make music]," he recalled to Zane Lo
for both Carla and Harry, then. Whe
feelings engendered by that encoun
another favourite S&G track he'd pl

Musically, "Carla's Song" revisits t
synth heartbeat underscoring a voc
then expands into something celebr
and the "waters" it crosses; backing
cymbals crash and when the track c
optimism. *Square One* magazine call
like the final track played before the

Carla was in the audience when S
in Manchester show on March 6. Be
graceful words. "Watching her disc
above everything else what a privile
through music. Carla, this one's for

Opposite: New York, March 15, 2026 – the day after he was both host and musical guest on Saturday Night Live.

COVER VERSIONS

"The guy can sing anything," *Billboard* magazine announced in March 2020. Anything ...and that includes cover versions – songs originally performed by other artists. Styles' career even began with one. Or, rather, two. Auditioning for *The X Factor* in July 2010, he sang "Hey Soul Sister" by Train, an upbeat pop-rock number that had been an American Top 3 hit the summer before. It only reached No. 18 in the UK, making it an unexpected choice for an audition song, but Styles went for it, singing along to – and being a bit overwhelmed by – a backing tape. Nonetheless, he roved the stage as if he owned it, which he did for 20 seconds. Then the music stopped and head judge Simon Cowell asked, "Can I hear something that's just you, without any music?"

Luckily, Harry had another one up his cardigan sleeve. His soulful take of Stevie Wonder's "Isn't She Lovely" got him through to the next round. And so it has continued: give Styles a good track to cover, and he'll put his distinctive stamp on it. That particularly goes for tracks that seem to be challenging choices, such as, say, Lizzo's "Juice". It's hard to imagine anyone successfully taking on this magnificent ode to self-love, but Styles did in Radio 1's Live Lounge in December 2019, and he absolutely inhabited the song. It required playfulness, which he exuded, and a vocal that ranged from warm and low to a downright NSFW "Ooooohhh!", both of which he supplied. When he reached the spoken part that advises "somebody" to fetch her boyfriend, who's been sending very personal direct messages to the singer, his delight at saying those lines was infectious.

Another unexpected choice, his version of Britney Spears' "Toxic", came about during one of his "Harryween" shows in New York in October 2021. This is one of those times when it's imperative not just to listen to but to watch the video: dressed as a clown, he marches up and down the stage catwalk, commanding the crowd to sing along.

It's possible that he didn't know Peter Gabriel's 1986 signature song "Sledgehammer" before he recorded part of *Fine Line* at Gabriel's Real World Studios in Box, Wiltshire. When he sang it on Howard Stern's SiriusXM radio show in March 2020, he said he'd picked it because of its Real World connection. Even if it was relatively new to him, his performance was remarkable – again, he got inside the song and brought his indie-rock A-game. (Gabriel retweeted a clip of the performance, adding clapping-hands emojis.)

His covers have erred on the side of classic rock, among which have been Joni Mitchell's "Big Yellow Taxi" on the Radio 2 breakfast show in February 2020 – he, keyboardist Charlotte Clark and guitarist Naomi Ludlow made an excellent harmony trio – and "The Chain" by one of his favourite bands, Fleetwood Mac. That one, included in a Radio 1 Live Lounge set in September 2017 a few months after the arrival of his debut solo album, was one of the first examples of Styles the Rock Star.

He does deviate from the classics from time to time, though. "Juice" and "Toxic" were surprising, but even more so was "Ultralight Beam" by Kanye West (now known as Ye), which he tackled at his debut solo gig at London's Garage on May 13, 2017. If there's a golden rule of covering songs, it has to be "Don't do a note-for-note copy", and Styles followed that rule. He skipped the original's rapped segments and sang the sung sections with the passion of a newly empowered solo artist.

Now he just has to add one of his covers to the tracklist of a future album...

Opposite: Styles opts for a striking fashion choice for an outdoor mini-set on the Today show. New York, May 19, 2022.

Overleaf: What a show! His first headlining weekend at Coachella. April 15, 2022.